THE BROOM IS OUT

Confessions of a
Budweiser Beer Drummer

DICK WALL

To David,
Best Wishes & thanks
for all of your help —

THE BROOM IS OUT

Confessions

of a

Budweiser

Beer Drummer

Dick Wall

DICK WALL

Leathers Publishing Company
Kansas City

THE BROOM IS OUT

PRINTED IN THE UNITED STATES OF AMERICA
ISBN: 0-9646898-1-2
Library of Congress Catalog No. 96-075895

Photograph Credits:
Negro Leagues Baseball Museum, Inc.—pg. 40
McDonnell Aircraft Corporation—pg. 154, 155
Anheuser-Busch, Inc.—pg. 162, 182, 229
Edward H. Goldberger—pg. 263
Dan Faron Studio—pg. 296
Ken Clark—dust jacket photo

Cover art by Cal Ennis.
Cover layout by DP Services.

Dedicated to

Mary Ellen

Who made so many sacrifices in her life,
To make mine so rich and pleasant.

Contents

Author's Note

This book tells the story of a beer drummer, a term I will explain in the Foreword. It unfolds against the backdrop of seven abiding themes: the author's family, his hometown of St. Louis, the Anheuser-Busch Company, radio broadcasting, World War II, McDonnell Aircraft and show business. All these topics played major roles in the author's life. The book developed out of stories told and retold in the course of rearing three sons, and of being a grandfather to their own children. Except for some jokes, the stories are true, and they come from my best recollection. As with everything in life, it is generally best to accentuate the positive. So unless I received permission to use their actual identities, I have changed some names, or slightly altered a few details, where incidents might show individuals in an unflattering light or otherwise embarrass them or their families.

This book is the product of effort by many people, and to each of them I give my deepest and most sincere thanks: to Joe Vaughan, an accomplished author in his own right, for his advice on how to approach the project; to my grandsons, Michael, Conor and Sean Wall, for giving me the inspiration and motivation to undertake it; to Alice Marie Bub and to Del and Jack McNamara for their excellent research assistance; to Dell Berry, Barbara Faubion, Barbara Gumminger and Margaret Dalke for their skill, good humor and hard work in typing the manuscript; to Sal and Cathy Calcara for their warm friendship and their special photographic help; to my good friend, Frank Nobrega, for his strong and steady support; to Darla Pennington for her skill as an editor; to my publisher, Tom Leathers, and his assistant, Barbara Thomson, for their confidence in the merit of this work; to my sons, Rick, Kevin and Terry, for their encouragement when my enthusiasm waned; and most of all to my beautiful wife, Mary Ellen, for her many fine suggestions, and for allowing me the time from our retirement to write this book.

It is my sincere hope that this "journey down memory lane" will give each reader a good sense of what it was like to live in St. Louis from 1920 through the 1950s, and to work as a beer drummer for Anheuser-Busch.

Foreword

In an age of market analysts, merchandising directors, advertising managers and sales consultants, the term *drummer* no longer means anything in the business world. It is used almost exclusively in this modern era to describe an individual who maintains the tempo in a rock band.

Before the birth of computers, however, *drummer* was the term for a person who worked a territory as a salesman. His job was to *drum* up business. I say *his* because, in those days, ladies generally did not work in such jobs. Whether the drummer worked locally or traveled coast to coast, which many of them did, his job was to make friends in order to retain and increase business. The drummer was often the only contact between his company and a buyer or purchasing agent. He could be in any field: hardware, soft goods, shoes or beer. Regardless, he was a drummer. Education wasn't important, and age was no problem. The drummer was successful if he understood his product and customers, knew his territory, and produced business for the company. This is the story of an Anheuser-Busch drummer, one of 25 or 30 people in the St. Louis branch for Anheuser-Busch in the 1950s. All of these people had different personalities and styles, but all were capable. We'll deal initially in generalities and later travel step by step through what was known as Territory No. 2 in St. Louis. But first we'll look at what brought one particular person to An-heuser-Busch as a drummer.

To tell the story, we have to start many years ago. In the beer business back in the '30s, '40s and '50s, it was the practice for each brewery to set up an incentive program for retailers. The brewery would set a figure, perhaps 50 cents, for each barrel purchased by the retailer. This amount was returned to the retailer on a monthly basis, but not in cash. Instead, the drummer would visit a tavern or saloon and spend the money credited to that outlet by purchasing samples of Budweiser for all those in the bar at that time. In other words, he would buy drinks for the house.

Now somewhere along the line, retailers began the practice of placing brooms outside the doors of their estab-lishments whenever the drummer was present. This was to advise all in the neighborhood that the drummer was in, and that drinks were free. As soon as the first person spot-ted a broom outside the door, word spread like wildfire. "The broom is out." In no time at all, the entire neighbor-hood was aware that drinks were free. All those who were interested then flocked to that outlet to sample grog pur-chased by the drummer. He purchased drinks until the amount which had been earned by this retailer was gone. He then would exit and be on his way to the next tavern, bar or restaurant in the neighborhood. There the scene would repeat itself. If your first thought is that some people would follow the Anheuser-Busch drummer all day, drink to their hearts' content, but never spend a nickel, you are absolutely correct. There were those who looked forward with great glee to the day someone would say, "The broom is out"—thus the title of this book!

The Old
Neighborhood

CHAPTER 1

Growing Up
on Wichita Avenue

If one must be born into poor or very modest, middle-class circumstances, Wichita Avenue in St. Louis was the perfect place to enter this world. There were better and certainly worse areas than the one in which my family landed, but we wouldn't have traded the old neighborhood for anything.

It was what politicians referred to as a melting pot. Irish, German, Italian, Greek and Jewish families made up our block. And the same nationalities could be found on nearby streets, such as Oakland, Cadet, Wise and Berthold.

Our family joined the Tobin, Kelly, Nolan and LaRussa clans at St. Cronan's Catholic Church at Boyle and Swan, about five blocks away. All of the Protestant churches in the neighborhood were well attended too. My sister Doris and I, along with other Catholics on the block, attended St. Cronan's School. Tuition there was one dollar per month. The children who went to public schools, either Stix at Euclid and Parkview Place, or Adams School at Tower Grove and Vista, paid nothing in tuition. These schools were tax-supported.

The old Manchester Theater (often referred to as the "Madhouse" by kids) cost only a dime. Many of us didn't worry about it, however. By delivering theatre circulars door-to-door, we were allowed to attend the movies as often as we liked, absolutely free. Benny Lieberman, whose father operated a shoe repair shop, delivered circulars with me. We did most other things together as well. We were so inseparable that John and Pat Brennan, who owned a grocery store at Taylor and Arco across from my grandfather's store, referred to us as "Richard the Irishman and Benny the Jew." Catholics were forbidden by Church law in those days to eat meat on Friday, so those of that faith also picked up the nickname "fish eater."

While most of the fathers in our neighborhood worked as policemen, firemen or laborers, some owned their own small businesses. Generally, they all seemed to have steady work. But I think my dad struggled more than most. As far back as I can remember, he worked in the food business. He was the assistant manager for Fred Harvey's Restaurant in Union Station at 18th and Market in St. Louis. He started with Harvey while still a bachelor. Shortly before transferring to the Fred Harvey's at Union Station in Kansas City, he married the lovely lady destined to become my mom, and they moved to Kansas City. Unfortunately, she didn't like it there. As a young bride with her family and friends 250 miles away, Mom was unhappy. So Dad asked for a transfer back to St. Louis, and they moved him home. But he told me many times over the years that it was never the same, and a promotion to manager of the restaurant never came. He often told me: "Never turn down a transfer."

In an effort to keep things going, Dad tried several types of work with the railroad. He also dabbled in local politics for a while before finally finding his proper place in life as the food manager at a rest home in Webster Groves. In the early 1950s, he and Mom opened one of the first modern nursing homes in the St. Louis area. They were getting a little old, however, and sold to younger people after two years. Dad died of cancer in 1956. Mom then moved in with my sister, Doris, and her husband, Bill Hagerty. She died of old age in 1968. Bill suffered a fatal heart attack in 1971, and Doris died a year later at the age of 55.

Dad was a big man, 6'2" and 185 pounds, but not particularly athletic. He was a hard worker, though. My mother, much smaller, was the personality kid. Everyone loved her. My Grandfather Wall, who was anything but warm or complimentary, frequently told us, "When Kate works in the dry goods store, business improves. Neighbors like to come in and talk with her, and when they do, they always buy something." Small wonder he liked her to fill in from time to time. Like most mothers, she was behind Doris and me in anything we wanted to do, just so long as it was honest.

Dad had always wanted to work for Anheuser-Busch. But it just never came to pass. He hoped, though, that I would some day go to work for the brewery. Although Dad was open to whatever line of work I chose, he felt strongly that I should become a brewery worker. It was good steady work, and Anheuser-Busch was a great organization. It treated its employees exceptionally well. But that thought was in the minds of most fathers in our neighborhood. "You'll always work. They never have a layoff, and the pay is better than average." Several of my parents' friends worked at the brewery. And their kids were the envy of the neighborhood because their dads worked at "Busch's," as it was popularly called at that time, whether as a bottler, electrician or painter.

From the age of 10 or 12, however, I wanted to be a radio announcer. I would read magazine ads from morning to night, imitating announcers of the day and dreaming that someday I'd get a chance to be on the air. My mom worked closely with me. She would listen and give individual attention, coaching me on style and pronunciation. In retrospect, I know she thought I was much better than I really was.

Every neighborhood had a baseball team. Jack Tobin, one of seven kids living right next to us at 4539 Wichita, was undoubtedly the best athlete around, and he pitched for our team. I was the worst player. But because I could get free baseballs from my grandfather's store, I was allowed to play right field. Football, soccer and baseball— we played them all. But we didn't play tennis, because we thought it was a sissy game. We even played corkball or bottlecaps (a game that originated in St. Louis). In both games, the batter used a broomstick and a tiny ball made of cork or bottlecaps.

Most of us learned to play golf. We gained all the experience we could while caddying at Triple "A" Club in Forest Park, or at Algonquin Country Club in Webster Groves. To this day, every time I see golf played on television, I think of the Harrison brothers at Algonquin, and of Benny Richter at Triple "A." They were the professionals at those clubs, and they encouraged all of us to learn the game while we worked as caddies. For our services we were paid 30 cents an hour, plus a chance to play on the course every Monday without charge. This exposure developed at least three fine golfers in our neighborhood: Virgil Bernson, Bill Vach and Maurice "Mush" Marshall. Mush also became well known throughout the St. Louis area as a great Irish tenor. Whether in a church, saloon or nightclub, Mush's voice was widely recognized and admired. I always envied him because I had a burning desire to be in the radio entertainment business. And he was always one step ahead of me. But whether it was golf, baseball, football or any other sport, all those activities took a back seat once we discovered girls.

At 4563 Wichita lived the Nolan family. The Nolan kids had lots of friends. So you can imagine what a party developed when the word went out that it would be "Nolan's on Saturday night." It seems that, in no time at all, the group of 15 fellows playing sports or shooting marbles dropped everything and responded with gusto.

Our home at 4541 Wichita was on a quiet street of only one block, between Kingshighway and Taylor Avenue. No matter where we were, it was always necessary to give specific directions to anyone wanting to know where we lived. "Two blocks north of Manchester Avenue and one block south of beautiful Forest Park" was one of the first things kids on our block learned to say. After all these years, those words still bring a warm thought to mind. I'm sure many of my friends from those days in the '20s, '30s and '40s share the same feelings toward what we still call "the old neighborhood." Though it has become a cliché, most of us in our neighborhood had little money. But it seldom was a factor in our lives. During our early years, we really had no need for it at all. Money wasn't plentiful but, as kids, we weren't aware of any severe shortages. For the most part, our mothers stayed at home and took care of the children, while fathers usually worked long days or nights. Most worked six days a week, and many of the women were forced to work from time to time, generally when the men were laid off or couldn't work because of weather.

Our home was no exception. As noted earlier, Grandfather Wall owned a dry goods store at Taylor and Arco Avenues, just three blocks from where we lived. This is where Mom clerked when it was necessary. When not working in the store, she prepared the three meals daily and accomplished all the other things that mothers and housewives generally did in those days. Either my sister or I would carry to the store a basket of hot food and a steaming bucket of tea that Mom had prepared. This ensured that Grandpa would always have a hot lunch. And although he was able to take care of the noon meal himself during winter months while Doris and I were in school, we carried meals often enough that some kids in our neighborhood used to call us "Little Red Riding Hood." It was a heavy schedule for my mother, but the old gentleman also owned the house in which we lived, so she didn't have much choice.

CHAPTER 2

School Days

After my graduation from Stix School, Mom and Dad began to stress the importance of education. There had been few high school diplomas (let alone college degrees) in our family, and they expected me to carry the ball in that direction. But I was so determined to get into some facet of show business that all of my parents' advice and encouragement had little effect on me.

Despite this fact, I generally received high marks on written tests, such as those administered by educational and business institutions prior to accepting a student or to offering employment. But books, whether educational or training materials, were usually not to my liking. I simply lacked desire in those areas.

On Labor Day following my completion of grammar school, however, Mom arrived home all excited with news that she had just come from a meeting with Father Dismas Clark, the assistant principal of St. Louis University High School. (This was the same priest later made famous in the feature film *Hoodlum Priest* for his ministry to death row killers and other criminal elements.) Father Clark had agreed to accept me as a freshman. Classes were starting the next day, and I must admit that I became excited to be going to such a fine school. And only a block or two from home! I was there the following morning—bright and early.

The Jesuits treated each of us with respect. But they let us know the "Jebbies" were in charge, and that things would be done their way. And so it was!

I tried—I really tried—to be a good student. But I soon was skipping school to attend live radio shows, and to meet some of the performers. They always seemed friendly. And despite my age, many of them even allowed me to attend rehearsals and to experience the thrill of what I perceived to be "Show Business." I became a "go-fer" at KWK and KMOX but soon was actually on the air for some studio and remote programs. I also received the almost unheard-of privilege of sitting in the radio booth for big league baseball at Sportsman's Park with Johnny O'Hara, Ray Schmidt and Allan C. Anthony.

But all of these thrills proved expensive. One fine day, Father Bill Bowdern, the principal of St. Louis University High, called me into his office. He advised me that my frequent absences were more than he would tolerate. Father Bowdern recommended that I try a public school, where perhaps they could discuss a program that would accommodate my desires.

I was shocked, but my parents were two steps beyond shocked. Although I had tried, I simply was unsuccessful at fitting in where "show biz" wasn't involved.

Without belaboring the point, I at least learned from my brief stint at St. Louis University High School that I had the ability to pass entrance exams. After passing a high school equivalency test in the Army, I was accepted following the war by three nationally respected universities. I eventually accumulated several years of college credits. Partially on that basis, several Fortune 500 companies, in addition to Anheuser-Busch, offered me employment.

Education finally found an appropriate place of importance in our family when my wife and I reared three sons. The oldest, Rick, graduated with honors from the University of Notre Dame and received a full scholarship to the Notre Dame Law School. He went on to enjoy a fine career as a lawyer. Today, he holds an ownership interest in Cerner Corporation, where he is Vice President, General Counsel and corporate Secretary. Our middle son, Kevin, majored in broadcasting at the University of Kansas. Today he is enjoying success as a network radio and TV sportscaster. Number three son, Terry, earned a psychology degree in three years at Rockhurst College and will soon receive an M.B.A. He presently is one of the senior executives for a federal investigative agency.

But I would never recommend the way I approached education. To all I say: Get your education and then pursue a career. But learn first!

The Old Gang

As the end of the '30s approached, our old crowd began to show more concern for jobs and marriage. And, yes, for the war in Europe, which many people felt would involve American troops. Lindy Nolan enlisted in the Navy. Bob Aulsburry and "Dingy" Fisher chose the Army, and all left the neighborhood. Soon the Nolan crowd began to diminish, as both fellows and girls seemed to be working or going to school in others parts of the city, where they developed new social acquaintances. One of the old songs we sang at the Beatty home while gathered around the piano was, "Those Wedding Bells Are Breaking Up that Old Gang of Mine." Those words were becoming increasingly true.

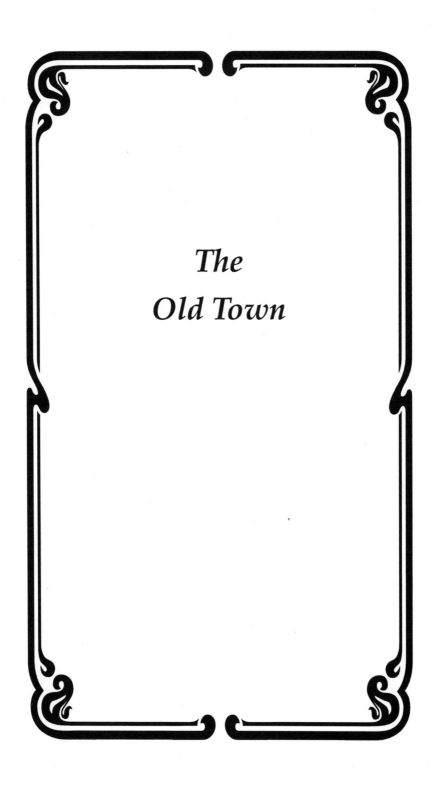

The
Old Town

A Brewer's City

André Malraux, I believe, once described St. Louis as "The Paris of the West." Both cities are indeed beautiful, with broad streets and exquisite architecture. Munich, however, with its many beer halls and fine breweries, is probably a more apt comparison.

Although beer drummers were active all across the country, St. Louis was unique in the beer industry during the first half of the twentieth century. Milwaukee had for years called itself the "Beer Capital of the World." But it was St. Louis, which once boasted more than 40 breweries (including some serving only local neighborhoods), that really deserved the title.

Shoe manufacturing was also big in the city. And for many years, the old St. Louis Browns baseball team played some of the "losing-est" seasons in sports history. To illustrate how well these facts were known to the rest of America, a cliché of the day was, "St. Louis: first in booze, first in shoes and last in the American League." Admittedly, that was establishing a reputation the hard way.

Because so many residents of St. Louis depended, either directly or indirectly, on beer as a source of income, the breweries became a great place to work. (That was and still is particularly true of Anheuser-Busch.) Salaries for brewery people were always better than in most other industries. And with working conditions and security better than one had reason to expect, the personnel office of the home of the "A/Eagle" was always busy.

I mentioned that, as a child in my middle-class neighborhood, anyone whose father worked at Busch's became the envy of every child on Wichita Avenue. This was true whether his dad worked in the actual brewing process, or as a drummer, maintenance man, painter, electrician or janitor. Busch took care of its employees, and layoffs were unheard of. So I grew up with the belief that anyone who wasn't in radio or some other form of show business, which was my first love, just had to work for Anheuser-Busch.

Printer's Ink

Just imagine! At one time St. Louis had four daily newspapers, covering an area and population smaller than the market now served by one paper.

As a result of sales, mergers and closings, the *Post-Dispatch*, the *Globe-Democrat*, the *Star* and the *Times* have become only one remaining paper today—the *St. Louis Post-Dispatch*. Ultimately, as in many other cities across the nation, newspapers lost much of their effectiveness, due in part to the improvement of radio and the arrival of television.

One paper for a city is not unusual today. Where in days gone by a large number of editors, reporters, "rewrite men," copy boys and other editorial and production people, along with an army of circulation workers, were needed to deliver four newspapers to a community, the modern publication now does the same job with a much smaller staff.

Sportswriters, for example, practically tripped over each other in the old days, with several covering the very same events. But the great writers who gained national recognition in the sports world while anchored at St. Louis include persons who will never be forgotten. J. Roy Stockton, Ed Wray, Sid Keener (who later became director of the Major League Baseball Hall of Fame), Kid Regan, Bob Burnes and Ray Gillespie are just a few of the great sportswriters enjoyed by readers in St. Louis and beyond. And there were many, many more.

Walker Cooper

If you followed St. Louis baseball during the '40s and '50s, you don't have to be briefed on Walker Cooper and his brother Mort. They were not only unusual as brothers who were teammates on a major league baseball club, but they were particularly notable because they were battery mates. In other words, Mort was the pitcher and Walker the catcher for the St. Louis Cardinals during the late '40s.

There are very few players who can make such a claim. John and Elmer Riddle, along with Wes and Rick Ferrell come to mind, but not many more. Mort's career was shorter than that of his brother, who played many years with the Cardinals and the New York Giants. Walker was known as a hard-hitting catcher. His lifetime batting average was .285. Mort won 128 games in 11 years, while losing only 45, with an ERA of 2.97.

I became personally acquainted with the Cooper brothers because of my radio work and because I bore a facial resemblance to Mort. I don't know how many times I was mistaken for him by fans, some even asking me for an autograph. But it was Walker ("Coop") whom I got to know very well.

If you have ever known a major league player, more than likely you've enjoyed many hours listening to inside stories of baseball. I certainly had fun with Coop. He had a real ability to tell a story, even though you just knew he was embellishing a little bit. Like the time he was discussing baseball announcers, and the name of Harry Caray came up. Now Caray has always been considered, if not the best announcer in the game, then certainly in the top two or three. But when Harry was doing the Cardinals games and Cooper was with the club, most would admit that Harry had a tendency to make the play a little more exciting than it actually was. Players and fans alike agreed on this. He would take a routine fly ball and describe it as a clothesline drive salvaged only by a sensational catch. But the fans loved it. I once told Coop, "No matter what anyone says, Harry describes a beautiful ballgame." Coop responded, "Yes, Harry does. We have a radio in the bullpen, and I must admit Harry describes a beautiful game. Only it's not the one we're playing."

The best Cooper story, though, involves the two brothers themselves and a famous slugger, Joe Medwick. Joe had been a star with the Cardinals before being traded. He was a notorious "bad ball hitter," but one feared by every pitcher in the league. And, for one reason or another, Joe was also sort of a loner. He never won the friendship of many players on the Cardinals or in the league. He didn't ask for favors nor did he give them. But he was a great star.

Most baseball fans at that time knew that Joe DiMaggio held the record for consecutive games in which he had at least one hit. DiMaggio's record was and still is 56 games in a row, with at least one hit in each of those games.

Medwick was traded to the Brooklyn Dodgers. He was moving toward a possible record when the Dodgers came to St. Louis to play the Cardinals. The fact is that he had not yet hit safely in 30 games. But he dreamed about breaking the record. In a game where Mort Cooper was pitching and brother Walker crouched behind the plate, Medwick knew his job would become tougher and tougher. Joe had been hitless in this game when he came up in the 9th inning for his final chance to get a hit and continue the streak.

Big Coop came out from behind the plate and asked brother Mort how he wanted to handle Medwick. Cooper said to his brother, "If he gets a hit, it will extend his streak. What do you think?" Both smiled at one another as Mort finally said, "Let's walk the son of a gun." With that base on balls, Medwick's chance of catching DiMaggio was gone. The two Cooper brothers quietly rubbed their hands with glee as they watched Medwick walk dejectedly to first base after losing all hope of ever surpassing DiMaggio.

CHAPTER 7

The Negro Leagues

In looking at St. Louis baseball, perhaps some would never think of segregated teams. It is important to remember, however, that, prior to 1947 when Jackie Robinson came up with the Brooklyn Dodgers, no black man had ever performed in the major leagues. So where did black players develop their talent in St. Louis? There were few blacks, if any at all, in the muny leagues. This left only sandlots in the black neighborhoods to serve as proving grounds.

But though it was impossible to play in the "big leagues," the top flight black players nevertheless had a place to play—and to receive pay for their services.

The Negro Leagues!

Yes, we've always heard about black teams from Kansas City, Indianapolis and other places, but St. Louis seldom is mentioned. And yet for years St. Louisans, black and white, had the St. Louis Stars as their Negro Leagues representative. They played home games Sunday afternoons in Star Park at Compton and Market Streets. And people paid to get in. How the two participating teams divided the pie, I really don't know.

But the black players were not only good athletes, they were great entertainers as well. Attending the games with my dad while still a boy was a great experience. Foremost in my memory is the picture of hundreds, and at times several thousand, black and white fans crowding into the stadium. Star Park wasn't the most comfortable in the land. But it offered not only good baseball, but prejudice-free baseball, plus hot dogs, peanuts and cold Budweiser.

Those black players were not necessarily household names in the white community during those days, but stars like "Satchel" Paige, John "Buck" O'Neil, "Cool Papa" Bell and "Smokey Joe" Williams were giant talents who packed the house whenever they appeared.

Buck O'Neil, a hard-charging first baseman for the Kansas City Monarchs, became one of baseball's top managers in the Negro Leagues. A very shrewd judge of talent, Buck later had a distinguished career as a coach and scout for the Chicago Cubs and Kansas City Royals, before becoming chairman of the board for the Negro Leagues Baseball Museum in Kansas City.

But more than in the big leagues, players in Star Park had real fun. They laughed, "rode" each other, and clowned, so that players and fans alike enjoyed themselves immensely. Naturally there were comparisons made. Would "Satchel" or Buck O'Neil make it in the big leagues? Of course! But the discussions were limited, because few white folks at that time ever imagined that a black man would one day play big league baseball. Talent wasn't the issue. It was pure discrimination. We will never know for sure how each one of the old Negro Leagues players would have fared. But it is enough to say that the quality of the big league rosters vastly improved after 1947.

John "Buck" O'Neil

CHAPTER 8

Drama Clubs

Although athletics played a big role for many of us, not all of the old gang participated in sports. Throughout the city, hundreds of young people were exposed to a mild form of the entertainment business through the many "Drama Clubs" which popped up. The Cathedral at Newstead and Lindell, Our Lady of Sorrows on South Kingshighway, and Visitation at Taylor and Easton were just a few of the Catholic parishes which offered singing, dancing and acting opportunities. These clubs attracted persons who were not necessarily interested in a show business career, but simply wanted to have some fun on an amateur level. Churches and schools of other denominations were doing the same thing. In no way did any of their productions rival the Little Theatre or similar programs. These were raw amateurs with an occasional appearance by a local "semi-pro" performer.

But among all of them, St. Cronan's Club was unique. We had everything necessary: an abundance of young persons who wanted to appear, a parish hall for rehearsals, and a member of the parish who was a professional musician to produce and direct. Dave Monahan, our producer and director, had been involved in the music program at St. Louis University. For several years, Dave had produced the very highly regarded "Purple Patches" at CBC High School. He was our "ace." He understood music and voices and how to put a show together. Plus he knew people.

Our plan was to do "reviews" rather than "book shows," which meant opportunities to use lots of people, without the worry of getting too deeply involved with narration and dialogue. It was called a Drama Club. But music and dance were our long suits.

Dave brought into our program a very talented choreographer to direct the dancers. Some of them were so inexperienced that "left foot, right foot" proved difficult. Charlene Powers knew dance. Her development of chorus lines, which turned out to be much better than we really expected, proved the point. Talented young ladies like Julie Saab, Mary Ann Dugan, Vera Beatty, Dorothy Nolan, Mae Logger and the Carrigan twins (Marcella and Marcia) were amazed at how proficient they became under Charlene's expert direction.

The "Boys" did some dancing, too, and a mixed chorus was an important part of every show. Grover Holmes was one of the MCs, and Rich Logger, Roy Schieszer, Bernie Dugan, Mel Shoults and Ed Strong were among the many talented chorus boys. Mush Marshall and Chick Mattingly were soloists. Mush and Chick were popular in shows all over town, but they came back each year to lend a professional touch to our extravaganza. All of the dancing and singing, which called for rehearsals three or four nights a week during a three-month period, were aimed at a specific audience, and the shows ran just two nights.

The only persons who would pay 35 cents to see our reviews were the mothers, fathers and other relatives of the cast, plus the boyfriends and girlfriends of the talent. So two nights plus a dress rehearsal were not bad at all. And the larger the cast, the larger the house. The musical reviews were admittedly less than professional. As I recall, they were *good.* But like others from the old neighborhood, our members eventually were drawn away by marriage, employment or world conditions. After three or four seasons, the company folded.

CHAPTER 9

Man of the Hour

I would be remiss to devote so many pages to St. Louis people and then not recognize the accomplishments of a man predicted by many to be "Most Likely to Succeed."

Our man of the hour is Herb Kaufman.

While never setting out to establish a record of any sort, Herb and his accomplishments in business, education and the humanities have proved impressive.

The son of Charles and Rose Kaufman, Herb and his brother, Bernard, spent most of their growing years in the family home at 1140 Boland Drive in Richmond Heights.

A graduate of Maplewood High, Herb then attended the University of Illinois. He returned to St. Louis after college, where he quickly showed signs of things to come.

A big and athletic man, Herb combined his physical stature with a warm personality that quickly won over most who met him. He learned early on that the most important part of any business organization is sales. And could Herb sell! He subscribed to the notion that the first step in selling is selling one's self. And Herb was right!

One of my friends, a sales executive, best described Herb Kaufman this way: "If I had but one chance to close a deal, if it had to be wrapped up right now, I'd want Herb Kaufman carrying the ball. He's a winner."

After surveying the many opportunities available to him, Herb entered retailing. Through the years, he combined his understanding of people with a sincere desire to advance in that competitive field of endeavor. As a result of great business acumen and lots of hard work, Herb rose to the pinnacle of success.

Top business people, of course, often receive opportunities in other parts of the country and in other industries. And in this respect, Herb was no exception. After all, if you are an exceptional salesman, you can sell anything! And opportunities came to Herb from several directions. One of them required a move to Las Vegas. Eventually, the entertainment industry attracted Herb's interest.

In 1980, Herb and *Tonight Show* host, Johnny Carson, became partners in Las Vegas-based KVVU - Channel 5. It subsequently became the No. 1 independent station in the country. Herb also owned and produced the "Boylesque Show" in Las Vegas for 15 years.

Herb Kaufman

With a national reputation in the television industry, Herb is now the largest stockholder in the Visitel Network, a Las Vegas-based company that operates television stations across the country. He also is the partner of Johnny Carson in a television production company, Kaufman-Carson Productions.

As the years rolled by, Herb Kaufman not only mastered the challenges of the business world, but also found time to serve as president of Temple Beth Shalom in Las Vegas. In the healthcare field, Herb for many years served as chairman of the board for Sunrise Hospital and Medical

Center, which is part of the largest hospital chain in the nation. And when any civic or charitable organizations in the vicinity needed help, they knew where to turn.

In addition to Herb's business and civic talents and interests, there is a musical side to him. Herb enjoys singing, and he is ready and willing to take the microphone whenever given the chance.

But the heart of Herb's life is his wonderful family. Herb married Irene Weisman, the beautiful daughter of Betty and Michael Weisman of St. Louis. Herb and Irene formed a lasting partnership that just couldn't miss. Her charm, steady hand and guiding influence in the life of Herb Kaufman certainly qualify her to participate in this recognition.

Living in Las Vegas for many years now, they have never lost their love for St. Louis. Their friends include many show business stars, U.S. astronauts and a number of political figures. But Herb and Irene still cherish their many friends from the old days.

Most important, however, is the fact that from this marriage came sons Jeff and Rick. Both are graduates of the University of Southern California and successful in their own right. So they may at some point be thinking of honors similar to those bestowed on their dad. But they know they have some pretty big shoes to fill.

CHAPTER 10

Let's Go
Down Memory Lane

Sports, entertainment, radio and newspapers head a list of people and places that appears endless. Make your own list and check it against this one.

Remember when you could:

- Shop in any of four downtown department stores: Famous Barr, Stix Baer & Fuller, Vandervoorts or Nugents. Stores in this beautiful downtown area were open Monday through Saturday, 9:30 a.m. to 5:30 p.m. (In wartime, they remained open until 9:00 p.m. on

Mondays only.) Incidentally, Famous announced its closing hour with a bugle call.

- Shop in stores where elevators were operated by sharply uniformed ladies who closed the doors only when so directed by the elevator starter.

- Enjoy an unbeatable chocolate sundae served in a silver sherbet dish by smartly attired ladies—all for only a dime.

- Receive assistance from a uniformed footman as your taxi or private automobile dropped you off at a department store.

- Get free next-day delivery to your home of items purchased at the store.

- Take advantage of specially priced items on "Dollar Day" sales.

- Ride buses or streetcars all over St. Louis on Sunday with a 25 cent pass.

- Ride in a service car limousine from St. Louis County to the Mississippi River for only 15 cents.

- Have four friends join you in a Yellow cab and all ride "for the price of one." The first 1/4-mile charge—35 cents.

- Enjoy a roast beef sandwich for a nickel on Big Bend Boulevard.

- Have lunch or dinner served in your car by a young carhop at Parkmoor Drive Inns all over town.

- Drive a bucket of golf balls for only 25 cents.

- Take an "all afternoon drive" to watch planes at the airport.

- See fabulous Muny Opera productions from the free seats.

- Enjoy a cold Bud plus the music of Maureen McCormick and Dick Balsano for 40 cents in the Walnut Room.

- Have a martini at DiMercurio's for 65 cents.

- See the Cardinals or Browns for $1.10, with kids in the "Knot Hole" gang admitted free.

- Have an auto dealer's instructor come to your home and teach you to drive, free.

- Pull into your neighborhood service station for gas and get complete service, which included vacuuming the inside of your car. A "fill-up" cost less than $2.00.

- Make a phone call for a nickel.

- Find an item in a dime store selling for a dime.

- Get a shoeshine for a dime.

- Get a custom-tailored suit for less than $30.00.

- Get a loaf of bread, packaged, for 5 cents.

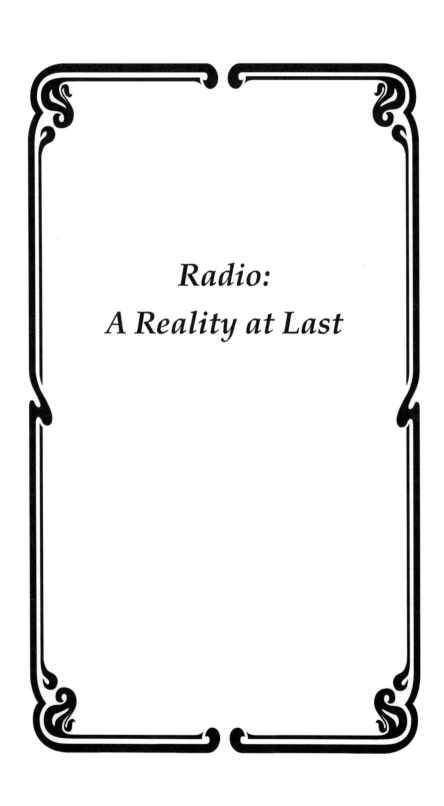

Radio:
A Reality at Last

CHAPTER 11

St. Louis Radio
in the Early Days

Radio in its early stages was a narrowly focused means of communication, information, education and entertainment. Deep-thinking business people quickly came up with the idea that radio signals could be directed toward millions of consumers, advising them as to how their lives would improve with the purchase of a specific product or service. Radio came alive!

The government, through the Federal Communications Commission or "FCC," accepted applications from individuals and business organizations seeking permission to establish radio stations. By the early '30s, several hundred stations were on the air, and advertisers were quick to jump on the bandwagon. The process was simple.

A station owner would take on the cost of establishment and maintenance of the outlet. He then would program music, sports, education, news, special events or anything else which would draw listeners. The station, for a fee, would then carry an advertiser's message as part of its programming. The more listeners the station's programming produced, the higher the fee. This was called *cost per thousand*, although that term is not used today as it was at that time. Much water has passed under the bridge since then, but radio station owners in the '30s and '40s realized they were onto something. Advertisers and their agencies found that, if their budgets didn't allow for radio, budgets would have to increase, or newspaper, magazine and direct mail budgets would decrease to allow for this new medium.

St. Louis, like many other cities, went for its share of stations. WEW, which was owned by St. Louis University, was first on the air, and others quickly followed.

While my dad kept urging me to work at Busch's, I continued to knock on the door of every radio station in town in hopes of becoming an announcer. In those days, there were many dramatic shows on the air. Some, like the *Land We Live In* and *The Pet Milk Hour*, were sponsored, and they used experienced performers. The story was the same in both dramatics and announcing. The question always asked was, "Any experience?" I knew the radio people, but I couldn't get a job.

Harry Renfro of KXOK, who later became a top executive in the advertising department of Anheuser-Busch, as well as Don Phillips of KMOX and Allan C. Anthony at KWK, were just a few of the good radio people I knew. Renfro one day gave me a tip on some public service programs being produced locally. They utilized the services of actors but had no budget for talent fees. I contacted Bob Shulman, who was a writer and producer for the Red Cross and other charitable agencies. He gave me a chance. For two years or more, I worked as an actor on KMOX, KXOK and WEW.

During this time, I also tried many non-radio jobs. I never let too many people know, however, because all of us working on radio shows wanted to be known as professional full-time performers. George Abel, who for years was the wrestling announcer on KSD-TV in St. Louis, worked with us in those early days. George once told me, "I would rather be an unemployed radio actor and announcer than employed in any other line of work."

CHAPTER 12

1930s and 1940s:
The Golden Era and KMOX

An old adage, "the worst two weeks in show business are Holy Week and a week in St. Louis," was also applied to a hundred other cities in this country. During the '30s and '40s, it was an inaccurate description of our city.

St. Louis in the '30s and '40s was an entertainment mecca. Television was in its infancy, but radio was on fire. In St. Louis, radio listeners chose a particular station and then stayed with it. KMOX, for example, was a 50,000-watt CBS outlet. It was the largest and most powerful station in the city, and it ranked number one in listenership.

KMOX was the leader, not only in programming but also in talent. Because it was owned by the Columbia Broadcasting System (the famous "CBS Network" of today), it found itself in the unique position of hiring the best in management and talent. It also paid top wages. In many cases KMOX found itself to be a network training ground for some extremely talented people. When the occasion presented itself, these local stars were able to move into New York and Hollywood positions. The chief announcer at KMOX, France Laux, was one of the top baseball and football announcers in the country. On many occasions in the '30s, he was selected as the play-by-play announcer for the World Series games, not only in St. Louis but throughout the nation. The station in those early days was located in the Mayfair Hotel. It later moved to the Mart Building at 12th and Spruce in St. Louis. The personalities who paraded through its doors each day were the very best.

Allan Roth was the musical director of this station. He conducted a 20-piece orchestra, not only for programs directed toward the St. Louis audience, but also on a daily basis to the Columbia Broadcasting System network stations all over the country. Vocalists included the great Russ Brown, who later left St. Louis to join the Jan Garber orchestra; Lorraine Grimm, who later appeared as the star of the Lucky Strike *Your Hit Parade* (but in those later days she used the name Kay Lorraine); Jack Norwine; Tom Baker; Bert Granville; and June Curran (who became June Curran Burton after her marriage). These were just a few of the outstanding singing voices heard over this station and the CBS Radio Network.

Hillbilly music was very popular in those days. Harry "Pappy" Cheshire and his group of more than 50 country musicians and singers entertained radio listeners from morning until night. Hillbilly music evolved into today's country and western. Cheshire, incidentally, was another of those air personalities who eventually moved to the West Coast, where he became a fine character actor in many Hollywood films. Older listeners will remember such great hillbilly personalities as Skeets and Frankie, Jimmy and Dick the Novelty Boys, Shucks Austin and the Texas Blue-bonnets. These were stars recognized not only locally but throughout the nation. So powerful and so successful were these country entertainers that many advertising executives throughout the Midwest believed that these people could sell *any* product on the radio broadcasts. Listeners could hear about the virtues of pet foods, cosmetics, farm implements and even automobiles.

Probably the most successful advertiser was a furniture store operator, Dick Slack. Dick was so enthused that he advertised on any station that carried hillbilly music. "Uncle Dick Slack" became a household name. Whether or not listeners were in the market for any of his furniture products, they at least knew who the sponsor was. The name Pappy Cheshire and announcer Don Phillips, along with Uncle Dick Slack, meant not only top-flight entertainment but good business as well.

With any list of KMOX performers goes the risk of missing some very talented people. One personality I cannot overlook was Marvin E. Mueller (later changed to Miller). He was a local boy who went from announcer and actor on KMOX to Chicago soap operas and top network announcing. Later a movie actor and star of the old *Millionaire* series on TV, Marvin was an indescribable talent.

Harry "Fuzzy" Gibbs, a personable actor seen by theatre audiences since his college days at Washington University, also appeared with the great Miss Tommye Birch and others in a family dramatic show sponsored by Pet Milk Corporation each Saturday morning. It originated in St. Louis but was one of many shows carried by the CBS Network. Al Chance, one of this country's best known radio producers, was in the control room for this show.

Harry later became "Texas Bruce" on a daily afternoon TV show—one of the first of its kind, and a show that brought him a large group of new young followers. Tommye had a tremendous voice and singing style in addition to her acting ability. She was very successful, not only in St. Louis but in Chicago with the Roger Pryor Orchestra at the Edgewater Beach Hotel, and later in Hollywood.

A very popular contemporary of Tommye, and also a KMOX regular, was a girl mentioned elsewhere in this book, June Curran Burton.

Studio orchestra director Allan Roth, like so many other members of this radio family, was recognized by the network bigwigs, who moved him to New York. Many CBS programs showcased the incredible musical insight of this talented man.

Roth was succeeded by Ben Feld, but only after a great search. Feld's arrangements served as accompaniment several times a week to the outstanding singing voices of Fredna Parker and Bert Granville. Granville was at home before a microphone as well as a nightclub audience. For many years, Bert was a singing MC at the old Jefferson Hotel's Boulevard Room, which featured top names from all over the country.

Lee Little, Maurie Cliffer, Johnnie Jacobs, Bob Dunham and Howard Dorsey were outstanding announcers who appeared on Bert Granville's shows, not only on radio but from time to time in his nightclub act at the Boulevard Room as well.

In addition to the "on air" talent at this CBS outlet on the banks of the beautiful Mississippi River, there also was outstanding talent in the production, sales and management sides. Most noteworthy was Robert Hyland, Jr. Bob was a native of St. Louis and the son of Dr. Robert Hyland, Sr., a nationally known physician and surgeon for the Cardinals and Browns baseball clubs. Bob Jr. was destined to be a tremendous success, not in medicine as his father had done, but in broadcasting. He started as an announcer, then worked for a while in sales. He soon became the vice-president and general manager of KMOX Radio as well as a vice-president of CBS. Bob brought new life to the advertising business in general and particularly to KMOX. His innovations in the area of talk and sports radio became textbook examples for other general managers all over the country. In fact, it is no exaggeration to say that Bob Hyland's impact on broadcasting is felt in the industry to this day.

CHAPTER 13

KWK

KWK, a 5,000-watt station, went on the air March 17, 1927. Its founder was Thomas Patrick Convey—a business-man and "on the air" personality. During the '20s and early '30s, he did play-by-play descriptions of Cardinals and Browns baseball. Not only was he St. Louis' number one fan, but he excited listeners all over the area with his trade-mark phrase, "And the score—oh, the score." But it made no difference whether the home team was winning or los-ing. It reached the point where fans used the phrase as a greeting. It became a household term.

The next baseball announcer on KWK was Bob Tho-mas Convey, the young son of the station's founder. Bob started when he was only 16, the youngest major league announcer in the country.

The list of sports people at KWK also included Ray Schmidt; Johnny O'Hara; John Neblett; and color announcers Jim Bottomly, a former first sacker for the Cardinals; Gabby Street, a major league catcher and manager; and one of the greatest color men St. Louis has ever known, "The Old Left Hander," Allan C. Anthony. Allan headed up an announcing staff that included Sterling Harkins, Martin Bowen, Bill Cook, Taylor Grant, Dick Fisher and others. They were what was known as "staff commercial announcers," not to be confused with "disc jockeys." Allan did it all, however: baseball, news, special events and straight commercial announcing.

While heading up the announcing crew at KWK, Allan also traveled each week to serve as the commercial announcer on the well-known network quiz program, *Dr. I.Q.* This program was heard every Monday night on the NBC Network. The Grant Advertising Agency produced it. Grant wisely decided that, by moving the program from town to town and originating it from larger cities throughout the country, the show would develop a greater audience than if it had been handled in the usual way. Lou Valentine created the program, and it was sponsored by the Mars Candy Company, which manufactured the famous Milky Way and Snickers candy bars. The program was tremendously successful, largely because it was different from many other quiz programs heard at that time. It is noteworthy that Allan Anthony was chosen for this announcing job after auditions by more than a hundred announcers throughout the country. He had a voice and style that really made listeners go out and purchase the advertised product—which, of course, was the reason Mars had sponsored *Dr. I.Q.* in the first place.

The disc jockey craze, which actually began with the "Make Believe Ballroom" in New York, caught on very quickly in St. Louis. Two major reasons for the popularity of "DJ programs" were Rush Hughes and Gil Newsome. Both were blessed with beautiful voices, and their interest in popular music bubbled across the airwaves. They developed tremendous listening audiences for KWK. A completely different approach to the task of audience building came from Myron J. Bennett ("MJB") and Ed Wilson.

Wilson was probably the greater performer. He not only had a flair for homey philosophy but also possessed a peculiar knack for "selling," particularly food products. If Ed recommended a product on the air, sales of that product would definitely increase.

Music from the network "big band" broadcasts filled the air most nights. But daytime and Saturday evenings brought KWK listeners a wide variety of music and songs. The broadcasts featured highly talented musicians—many of whom were so in demand that they kept busy at nightspots, in addition to radio jobs during the day. Tony DiPardo, Rolla Coughlin, Al Sarli and others led the studio band from time to time, and all were highly respected in the music world. Some of the singers were Harry Babbit, his brother Gene, Bill Foreman ("the old top notcher"), Tommye Birch (who also sang on KMOX and KSD), Peggy Duncan, Coyita Bunch, Alan Dale and, of course, June Curran Burton. Other talents came and went, as was the case on all broadcasting stations. But KWK was justifiably proud of its roster of entertainers, most of whom had long-term "staying power."

Not to be outdone by other stations, KWK's staff also included "The Range Riders," a quartet which for many years provided listeners with some of the most outstanding hillbilly and country western music. They were very popular in St. Louis but were also known throughout the country as a very successful and talented group. With it all, St. Louis found in KWK a station which provided sports, music and comedy to an audience throughout the Midwest. In most instances, KWK relied on music to develop listeners. The only exception to that rule was the *Ed Wilson Show*. In order to build an audience, Ed depended more upon his ability to talk than on featuring popular songs. Ed once remarked that he didn't try to play the top tunes. He left that up to Gil Newsome or Rush Hughes, or to the live orchestra. Danny Seyforth, the director of production for KWK, once remarked that Ed Wilson could play "Come to Jesus" and still win a large audience. Wilson depended primarily on his ability to communicate verbally, with music being only a small part of his act.

Gil Newsome had a format similar to that of the Lucky Strike *Your Hit Parade*, in that he selected music for his program based on the sales of records each day, with information supplied by several local record stores. If record sales were high, that meant listeners were interested in those particular tunes, so Newsome offered that same music to his radio audience.

KSD

KSD, owned and operated by the *St. Louis Post-Dispatch,* served as NBC's outlet in St. Louis. Its studios were at 12th and Olive Street. In view of such ownership, it was predictable that KSD would be strong in news. George Burbeck, its general manager, was an excellent radio man. He operated a station well balanced with news, music and sports, in addition to a heavy network schedule.

Hod Gram was KSD's program director, and he also appeared on the air as a sports man. The staff was made up of pure commercial announcers. Frank Eschen, a dependable and knowledgeable man who could do studio work with precision, was at his best on special events, such as parades. John Roedel, with a deep and resonant voice, was so good that, when TV came in, he made the transition with ease and became a most dependable news anchor. Max Cole was another steady performer who later appeared in several Hollywood films. Del King and Willard Scott (he should not be confused with a personality of the same name who later built quite a following as the weatherman on NBC's *Today* show) were others who contributed to this first-quality staff.

Russ David, a pianist with uncanny ability, was the musical director who performed daily on the station. His musical knowledge and good taste were combined with excellent management to bring St. Louis a great radio station. Russ was not as promotion-minded as some, and he permitted no screaming commercials under his direction. KSD just exuded class.

CHAPTER 15

KXOK

KXOK went on the air in the mid-'30s. Its owners, the *St. Louis Star-Times*, found a dedicated and serious radio man to serve as general manager. He was Chet Thomas, a man who had an unusual combination of youth and experience, as well as a knack for selecting the right person to fill each job. Harry Renfro served as an assistant to Thomas and directed the news department with great skill.

Bob Hille, Bob Lyle, Alex Buchan and Bob Shea headed up the talent list, which shouldered the news-music-sports format quite well and developed a strong listening audience.

Major league sports were constantly on the station's drawing board, a factor that eventually saw Harry Caray (his real surname was Carabino) on the staff. The news, sports and music programming gave Renfro and Hille a chance to do what were called "remote broadcasts." Mikes were set up in nightspots around town, and the live music was sent across the airwaves of KXOK. Harry and Bob produced and announced their shows from the "Walnut Room" in the old Gatesworth Hotel and the "Tune Town Ballroom." KXOK made St. Louis proud.

WTMV

In addition to what was referred to as the "top four" St. Louis radio stations, 250-watt WTMV in East St. Louis must receive mention. It was WTMV that gave me my first professional announcing opportunity.

I had made the rounds of radio stations again and again, but it was Harry Coleman, program director of WTMV, who called and said, "I can give you $20 a week plus all the sporting event and theatre passes you can use, if you want to join us." This was in 1938. It didn't take but 30 seconds to accept that offer, and I was at last "in radio" on a full-time basis.

Before long, I became chief announcer and sports director. Of course, I was with a small station. But it was in the St. Louis market! It has been said a thousand times that, in small stations, you get a chance to do everything. And it is true.

But those chances were opportunities! Play-by-play sports—news—dance remotes—"man on the street" interview programs—studio music shows—a chance to sing: it was all there!

Dick Wall broadcasting on WTMV in 1938.

A very talented and popular pianist, Bill Hart, entertained nightly for many years at the "Olde English Inn," an East St. Louis nightspot. During the day, he served as musical director at WTMV, which meant he performed live in daily radio shows. And he gave me a chance to sing with him on the air. I enjoyed it—and got paid too.

I mentioned earlier that hillbilly music was popular at that time, and the biggest sponsor in the area was "Uncle Dick Slack, the Jolly Irishman." He sponsored two half-hour shows each day on WTMV, featuring a popular local group, "Suzy and Her Sons of the Ozarks." I was the commercial announcer, and Suzy let me sing too. Working with talented people like John O'Hara, Ray Schmidt, Roy McCarthy, Byron Scott, Alan Walker, Jack Norwine, and one of the first women to work "on air" in the St. Louis market, popular personality Jackie Straight—well, it was all great fun.

WTMV was good to me. I had those great opportunities—to announce, to sing, and to do everything I always wanted to do.

The highlight of it all occurred when I successfully auditioned for the "Wheaties" people and thought I would be doing professional baseball in 1942. The tragic events of December 7, 1941, however, altered my plans, as well as those of millions. The early days of 1942 brought changes in many radio stations. Ours was no exception.

General managers Carlin French (who was there before the war) and Mike Henry, who followed, made the job very easy. I stayed with them until joining the Army, and then returned to WTMV after the war.

CHAPTER 17

Dizzy Dean and Me

Earlier I wrote that I was the worst baseball player in our neighborhood, and that I was allowed to play right field on our team because my grandfather owned a dry goods store where I could get free baseballs. Why, then, do I expect anyone to believe me when I talk about playing on a team in old Sportsman's Park with such star names as Dizzy Dean on the mound and Gabby Street behind the plate? And imagine losing the game!

For several years, back when St. Louis boasted of two teams—the Cardinals in the National League and the Browns in the American—it was the custom at that time to stage a ballgame in the big league park on the last day of the season, prior to the final big league game scheduled for that day. The St. Louis area radio reporters would play the local newspaper sportswriters.

On this day in the late '30s, when the Cleveland Indians were in town to play the Browns, the starting time of the regular season game was moved back, with a media game scheduled for 12:30 p.m. The game was to be concluded after an hour and a half—if the players could last that long. I, of course, was on the broadcasters team. We were the home club, wearing the extra home uniforms of the Browns, and we sat in the third base dugout. The newspaper team wore the road uniforms of the Browns and used the first base dugout. There were no tryouts for the teams. One had only to be in the broadcasting business and show up at game time. We used the big league umpires, three of them at that time, and they got into the spirit of this farce.

Crowds were very small for the Browns in those days, especially on the last day of the season. But the few hundred who bought tickets indicated that this exhibition game was a larger attraction than the Indians and the Browns. Because we were the home team, the radio announcers took the field first. I played third base, from WTMV. But beyond that we were a powerhouse. Imagine France Laux, of KMOX, first base; Johnny Neblitt, KWK, second base; Johnny O'Hara, shortstop; Bob Hyland, left field; and Alex Buchan, KXOK, center. Ray Schmidt, KWK, was our rightfielder and coach, under manager Gabby Street who, of course, caught, and Dizzy Dean, pitcher. Diz had starred with the Cardinals and later was injured in an all-star game. After being traded to the Chicago Cubs from St. Louis, he retired and began broadcasting the Browns and Cardinals games. Diz, of course, was not in playing condition. But at his worst, he was head and shoulders above everyone except Bob Hyland, who had been a great player at St. Louis University. (Incidentally, Bob was selected as the star of our "exhibition" game.) Of course, Diz didn't display any of the speed he had shown years before. But then he simply tossed toward the plate, and nobody hit him very hard anyway. Strikeouts and pop-ups were the mainstay of this game, although one of the writers hit a fly ball into left center, which Hyland raced for and handled like a big leaguer.

We broke into a 4-0 lead, and by the third inning Diz was growing weary. He said he would rather sit in the radio booth and talk than go back to work. I mentioned earlier that the major league umpires worked the game. So, before checking out, Diz decided that if the fans wanted to see the real thing, we'd make them happy. He, John Neblitt and I gathered in the corner of the dugout and waited for the umpire to call a strike. As he did, the three of us, at Diz's urging, stormed the plate to dispute the call in big league fashion. The fans loved it and, small as the crowd was, they were all on our side. In only a few seconds, the plate ump's right hand went up, and Diz was gone, kicked out of the game. He delayed leaving, however, and kicked dust toward the umpire while the fans howled.

Our hitter at the plate finally struck out, and the inning was over. Diz had stayed in the dugout, but since we had no other pitcher—and in the spirit of the occasion—the umpire let him return to the mound. Soon our 4-0 lead was reduced to 4-3, and strange things were happening. Out of the first base dugout came some hitters whose road uniforms were not exactly complete. It turned out that some of the Browns' regular players were quickly borrowing shirts from the writer's clubhouse, donning them, and stepping up to the plate to hammer our pitcher. Diz found himself now pitching to real big league players, most of them much younger than he was.

The final score: we lost 7-4, and I didn't get a hit. But hey, I didn't promise a pennant contender, simply a game where I played on the same team with Dizzy Dean and Gabby Street.

CHAPTER 18

Radio Wrap

Records of talent and programming information are not available in most cases, so the details of "who was where" are largely a result of the author's memory. If I failed to mention some person who lived and worked in this era, I apologize. The truth of the matter is that many who never worked on the staff of the top four stations nonetheless played a part in '30s and '40s radio.

Talented people like Hans Kolmar, Jim Riley, Johnny Yates, Bev Watson, Dale Douglas and George Abel, among others, were constantly attending auditions or interviews in an effort to "break into" or to remain in radio. Some gained local employment, some left town for work, while

others landed spots in stations other than the network outlets.

It was a fabulous era in a wonderful industry!

Hey, I've Been Drafted!

CHAPTER 19

You're in the Army Now

While waiting to be called to service, I continued air work, including "game shows" and other programs involving uniformed service people. This was in addition to my regular duties at WTMV.

At that time, the possibility that I could obtain a position in the St. Louis office of the U.S. Marine Corps evaporated when I measured 6'7" tall, which exceeded the maximum height limit in that branch of service. But the time eventually came for me to join millions of others who heard the call. March 7, 1942, saw me reporting to Jefferson Barracks in St. Louis.

Within a few days, I had been inducted, outfitted, and assigned to a pool which included men from all across the Midwest. They soon enough would be scattered around the country, with little regard for background, education or preference. The main criterion appeared to be assignment where "bodies" were needed to fill the basic training centers.

I could have been sent to any one of more than a hundred camps, but Fort Lewis, Washington, was my draw.

Basic training for me started with the Medical Corps. That's right, the Medical Corps! By May I was on my way to Australia, but in the weeks prior to this I received basic training at Fort Lewis along with hundreds of other new soldiers, some from St. Louis and the rest from other parts of the country. Our training was roughly the same that others in the military received. At least we knew we would be through for the day at 5 p.m. and free to pursue any interest we chose.

During my three months at Fort Lewis, I spent the evenings searching for some opportunity to use my limited radio experience, with a hope that perhaps I could get into the entertainment, special services or radio branch of the Army. I learned that there were radio programs produced right on base at Fort Lewis, and I inquired as to how I might participate. Not only to use what experience I had, but also to pick up additional experience, which would help me after the war was over. I auditioned for the people in charge of a weekly radio program that originated from the Post Theatre. It was designed not only for listeners throughout the area but also for members of the military who were seated in the audience. I was accepted.

I had the privilege of working with many experienced people and performing on a variety of shows produced and directed by Sgt. Howard Duff—the very same actor from Hollywood. He not only was talented but was also more than willing to help other people in the business. Howard later drew duty in Hollywood as an Army sergeant but became a big TV and movie star after the war. In just a few months of working with Duff and others, I gained experience that one could never buy.

I shall always remember the day that we were preparing to produce a program in the Post Theatre with about 300 GIs in the audience. I didn't realize what my part would be in this program, and it was Howard Duff who turned to me about ten minutes before air time and said, "You do the warm-up." I didn't really understand the term, but he quickly told me that it would be my job to go out and stand before the audience of 300 and tell them some jokes to relax them and literally "warm them up." Because I had experience as an MC, I quickly reached into the back of my mind and told three or four stories to the soldiers sitting out front. Not only was this a great opportunity, but it also gave me experience working before an audience, a skill that helped me during the rest of my days in broadcasting.

As the weeks rolled on, I envisioned this as a steady job within the Army. The word soon came, however, that my unit, the medical unit in which I took basic training, was shipping out. My Fort Lewis radio career was coming to an end. But before we packed our gear and boarded the USS *West Point* as medics sailing to Australia, we had one more training class to attend.

Because this was Medical Corps Basic Training, we experienced close order drill, ten-mile hikes, physical fitness and all the other things included in every soldier's life. We also learned things that would be helpful if we were actually assigned to a medical combat unit after basic training—how to treat a battlefield wound, how to take temperatures, how to apply a bandage, how to read blood pressure measurements, even giving a bed patient his bath.

Now we were approximately 500 men in this outfit. Probably not more than 25 would ever be called on to bathe a patient, but the entire group was ordered to observe how it should be done. We were all seated in the Post Theatre, where an Army nurse was to address us on all the steps involved in giving a bath. The 5'2" blonde must have been the most beautiful girl in the Nurse Corps. When she walked onto the stage and asked for a volunteer "patient," she drew whistles and catcalls from many in the audience who had been civilians just a few weeks before.

And in every camp, of course, there was one GI who was the "clown," the one who could always be trusted to give everyone a laugh through his wisecracks and general behavior. Ours was Jim Cavanaugh, a friendly young Irish lad from north St. Louis, where he later operated a saloon at Kingshighway and Natural Bridge. Naturally, as the young nurse asked for a volunteer, the cry went up from the crowd, "Cavanaugh, Cavanaugh." After only a few moments, Jim approached the stage, eyeing the pretty nurse and winking to the crowd.

She asked Jim to lie on a bed on the stage, as though he were a patient who could not get out of bed but needed a bath. She explained the procedure: first wash the left arm, left leg, and so on. As Cavanaugh and the audience observed, they simultaneously anticipated what would happen next, as the beautiful young nurse approached the more private parts of Cavanaugh's anatomy. None of us could really believe what was going to occur, but we anticipated the inevitable. Slowly, the nurse took a face cloth and narrated, "Take the left arm and wash toward the shoulder as far as possible. Now the right arm, and wash as far as possible. Now start with the left leg and wash up as far as possible, now the right leg and wash up as far as possible."

Then the blood pressure of all 500 soldiers in the theatre, including Jim Cavanaugh, rose as they waited for the beautiful young nurse to reach toward Jim's more private parts. She turned, looked at the crowd, and then back to the patient. She, of course, brought the house down as she tossed the cloth back to Jim and said, "Now you wash 'possible.'"

CHAPTER 20

If the Shoe Fits

With the cost of a shoeshine at your local barbershop running $3 or more today, it may be difficult to imagine that not too long ago (in the '30s and '40s) the going price for a first-class shoe service (including saddle soap, polish, brushing and soft cloth treatment, topped off with a whisk broom dusting of your clothing) ranged from 10 to 25 cents.

I mention this only in recalling that Elmer Gallard, considered by many at the time to be "Mayor" of the Euclid and Laclede area in St. Louis, was a strong advocate of "Shoeshines for All." He felt shoeshines were important because, "If your shoes look good, the rest of your clothes look even better." But it's apparent today that the improvement in leather and shoe manufacture has seen shoeshines on the wane.

Nevertheless, upon entering the Army in World War II, I learned that a shoeshine was more important than Elmer Gallard ever dreamed.

Frank Gianetti was a textbook platoon sergeant. He had the appearance, the style and the voice of a sergeant whose job it was to mold a group of Army recruits into 40 trained soldiers in a matter of weeks at Fort Lewis, Washington. He accomplished his goal by showing a personal concern for each young man in his charge, paying close attention to even the smallest detail.

In my case, it was a pair of GI shoes. Everyone entering the Army was supposed to be issued two pairs of shoes. One was to be used for basic training duties—hiking, drilling, and so on. The second pair was to be worn at higher class affairs, both on and off the base. The "dress" shoes were to be highly shined so that they could be worn, among other places, at "retreat," the final military function of each workday.

Because I wore a size 13 shoe, the supply people said they had only one pair for me. They would have to put my second pair on special order. As a result, I wore my size 13 shoes all day long, in water, dirt or what have you, and continued wearing them in the evening, while others slipped into their highly polished pair after 5 p.m. Despite my efforts to keep this only pair of shoes in fairly nice condition, Sgt. Gianetti was upset. He reminded me each day that, regardless of problems, my shoes should be shined at all times. He gave me special advice and instructions to no avail. In desperation, he gathered our platoon in a circle one evening and pointed to me as an example of how any situation could be corrected if we really worked at it.

He asked for my right shoe, which I slipped off and handed to him. Then, with 40 men looking on, he started a series of scrubbing, buffing and polishing actions that anyone could see was improving the appearance of that scuffed shoe. It was a slow but effective process. As I saw what was happening, the price of a civilian shoeshine came to mind. I began to smile a little as I nudged a friend and said, "Even though I'm the subject of Gianetti's lecture, it's worth it. Where else can I get a shoeshine for free? This is a real gift."

The sergeant finished his hard work and, as he held my shoe in the air so that we could all see the mirror-type shine, he said, "See what can be done if we work at it!" I continued to smile, thinking I had just saved 25 cents.

Sgt. Gianetti then tossed the gleaming shoe toward me and said, "Here, Wall, now you make the other one match it!"

CHAPTER 21

Journey Overseas

When a young man begins an overseas journey during wartime, he is overtaken by one or more of several emotions: loneliness, fear, pride—to mention just a few. In my case, it was primarily loneliness, with a touch of pride. I knew I was leaving a family of loved ones. I was lonely and concerned with the uncertainty of where I was going, and when and if I would ever come back.

But after the weeks of basic training, I boarded a train for San Francisco. In those days, San Francisco meant "overseas" to anyone in service.

But when our group began to board the *West Point*, a converted luxury liner, I realized I had acquired a new family. Not only my fellow members of the 105th General Hospital, but some 6,000 other travelers who made up our passenger list.

Our group included people like Ray Steitz and Jack McCarthy, who were talented young lawyers fresh out of St. Louis University, and Sammy Marcus, another fine lawyer who had just graduated from Washington University. Others included Gene Ahlert, Jim Cavanaugh, Tom Lawler, Paul Billy and many more who were destined to become good friends as we sailed on May 19, 1942. While many on board had duties assigned to them, most of us were free to rest and talk with others, all of whom were as much in the dark as we were, trying to imagine what was in store for us.

CHAPTER 22

Abandon Ship

When a soldier boards a "Troop Ship," he isn't furnished with a brochure containing details of what is to come on the "cruise." He is given a place to sleep, perhaps space for his barracks bag, and little else. Rumors will fly but, unless the GI has a unique connection, his information will be limited to almost zero. For example, on the *West Point* on which I sailed from San Francisco, we were told only where we slept and nothing more, not even what our destination was to be.

I learned early in our journey that a chief petty officer from St. Louis was the most reliable source of information that I could locate. If I heard a rumor, I would check my source for verification at the first opportunity. Even then, one waits for "important" rumors before inquiring. One of the first things to disturb me was the fact that, although we were sailing through Pacific Ocean waters that were infested with Japanese submarines, we were not part of a convoy! Why not? Here we are, 6,000 soldiers with nothing but water in sight, and not a friendly ship to be seen. It was scary. Especially for a guy who didn't even know how to swim!

Now I wasn't very knowledgeable on the ways of the sea. But the justification for our situation, as explained by those who should have known, well, let's just say it left some room for additional explanation. The best we could learn was this: "The *West Point* is the largest ship afloat," and therefore capable of doing things the enemy could not overcome. U.S. intelligence apparently reported that Japanese submarines needed a period of perhaps six minutes to aim and fire their torpedoes, so our ship changed its course every five minutes, making it possible for the *West Point* to steam alone without convoy. As much as I believe in my country, I tell you it was with some uncertainty and trepidation that I stood on deck of the *West Point* with nothing but water as far as I could see.

My next concern was the location of my sleeping quarters and the effect that Navy rules would have on them. There are two warnings that actually demand participation of all on board. "Battle Stations" was called with the ringing of bells throughout the ship. This signal ordered all passengers to stop what they were doing and to allow sailors to have the right-of-way. Then all aboard were required to report to specially designated areas deemed critical during an emergency. Although we never encountered a real emergency, test drills occurred from time to time.

But the most important drill of all was "Abandon Ship," which the crew signaled with sirens and bells sounding throughout the ship. The difference from the earlier warning was that, in this drill, sailors reported to their assigned stations, while passengers were instructed to return to their bunks so that lines could be formed and a calm abandonment of the vessel effected. I was living on deck "C," which meant that, along with hundreds of others, I was below water level. A frightening thought! The first drill found most of us on higher decks, meaning we had to rush to our below-water-level bunks to line up so that we could slowly march to the top deck. After about one hour, we had progressed only 40 or 50 feet, and soon the drill was cancelled.

One need not be a Rhodes scholar to figure out why the lines moved so slowly. The first in line didn't really "abandon ship." No one actually went over the side, so those of us at "C" deck couldn't move up. It was a theoretical drill, but you can bet the farm that when the second "Abandon Ship" command was ordered several days later, I was on deck "B," where I conveniently "forgot" and went directly topside.

CHAPTER 23

Down Under

Those 17 days on the Pacific Ocean (depending on whether or not you counted the equator crossing) brought us closer than we had anticipated, as 12 soldiers shared a stateroom which had previously housed only two guests during the glory days of luxury cruising. We arrived in Melbourne, Australia, on June 4, with wide eyes and an eagerness to start our new life "down under."

We set up camp in Yoronga Park, across the street from Melbourne University, and for two weeks combined minimal work with a great opportunity to meet the natives and learn the ways of our hosts.

The Australian people were wonderful. They offered to buy us drinks in the pubs and even invited us into their homes, where we learned what hospitality really meant. Some of our people met young girls and saw acquaintanceships grow into love. Obviously, we had no weddings during our first stay in Melbourne. But several people I know either married before leaving Australia for good, or they came back after the war, following their discharge in the States, to go down the aisle.

Soon we received orders to move out, and our troop train rolled through beautiful cities, towns and farmland, delivering us days later to the rural town of Gatton. Gatton was the home of a fine agricultural college, which had converted in wartime to a general hospital operated and controlled by the United States Army. The hitch was that we had to do the converting ourselves. From the yardbird level to completion, our outfit constructed a first-class, 500-bed hospital unit. Following completion of the medical center, many of us were assigned to duties different from those we had previously known. I worked as clerk for the Catholic chaplain, Father John Murphy, another St. Louisan. Father Murphy had served as parish priest at the "Rock" church on North Grand Avenue before the war.

Not only was the work enjoyable, but it gave me a chance to use my spare time working with a local radio station, 4BC in Brisbane. Brisbane actually was about 90 miles from Gatton, but our motor pool and the Aussie Railroad made it possible to travel to nightspots where music and dancing went on seven evenings a week.

The streets of Brisbane, a city with 300,000 at that time, were jammed with activity. The department stores, restaurants and theatres enjoyed a five-fold increase in business over what they had experienced in prewar days. Some of our people were stationed permanently in the city or at nearby camps, but most of us were prepared to move "up north," where the New Guinea and other island fighting was growing more fierce by the day.

Army, Navy, Marine, Air Force and Merchant Marine personnel filled the streets and sidewalks, ready to spend money and enjoy each day and night, trying not to dwell on the orders to move up, which they knew would come without warning. New Guinea wasn't far away.

General MacArthur

Long before I ever dreamed of serving in the military, my dad had told me about General Douglas MacArthur. Many stories of his West Point career and some of the controversy he experienced in his military life prompted me to remark to my dad: "If I'm ever in the Army, I hope I get to serve under General MacArthur."

Several years later, despite some derogatory references made about him by the press and by a few officers under his command, I was excited to learn that the General had established headquarters in Brisbane, Australia. While I had never before seen MacArthur in person, it would have been hard not to recognize him.

It's obvious that the highest ranking officer in the Southwest Pacific area would seldom window-shop or have coffee at the corner cafe. First, his job was both difficult and time consuming. Second, he had tremendous responsibility, and then there was the concern for his safety.

The hotel that housed field grade and general officers in Brisbane was located just off Queen Street in the downtown area. Headquarters of the United States Armed Forces in the Far East, which General MacArthur commanded, was located in a building four blocks away. Commuting between these two structures was done in a well-guarded staff car, which meant the General was seen on the street infrequently.

Specially trained Military Police guarded the General, his family and their quarters in the Lennon Hotel. Mrs. MacArthur and their five-year-old son, Arthur, were protected in much the same way as the President's family, both in their apartment and during travel and recreation. One of the finest M.P.'s assigned to the special unit was a former minor league baseball player, Milt Katzman, from Chicago. He and I became great friends. As a result, Milt invited me to see the MacArthur apartment on the Lennon's third floor. Milt was on "third floor" duty when I entered the hotel to see the quarters, and I assumed that the General was not at home. With the OK from a lobby guard, I entered the elevator, which was already occupied by two majors. I pressed "number three" and waited.

I didn't know that young Arthur was interested in music, so I was particularly surprised to hear the sound of drums floating down from above. As the door opened, I stood at attention as the two majors began to exit. To the shock of all aboard, our five-year-old drummer broke into a combination of snare and base drum beats accompanied by cymbal clangs. His equipment had been set up within inches of the elevator door!

The majors tried to maintain their balance but tripped over the drums, harming no one, but spreading kettle drums and bells all over the room. Suddenly emerging from an adjoining room, was a striking military figure. Here I was face to face with General Douglas MacArthur! Clad in casual clothes, the General appeared to place concern for safety of the lad at the top of his priority list.

He seemed hardly aware of the presence of enlisted men in the room. As he reached down to lift the little boy from the musical rubble, the great military commander said proudly to the officers, "I don't care what he does, gentlemen, just so he becomes a good soldier."

As we prepared to leave the apartment, I couldn't help but think of my dad. How proud he would have felt at that moment. Not only did the kid from our old neighborhood get to serve under MacArthur, as millions did, but he was able to meet him in his apartment home.

CHAPTER 25

Special Services

After several months of commuting, I was transferred into Special Services to work more closely with military and civilian people in Brisbane. Through my duties in a Special Services Unit, I found that there were no hard feelings toward those remaining behind on the part of those who were soon to move up to the jungle. On the contrary, our men and women packed the halls where the 32nd Division band played, and where the "Base Section 3" band sounded off each night. These bands played for dances, because dancing meant girls, and that brought smiles to the faces of GIs. The community building and Red Cross facilities were the scenes of entertainment almost every night. Bill Walker, who played with big bands before and after the war, headed up the 32nd Division band. It was acclaimed by visiting musicians Artie Shaw and Little Jack Little to be as fine as any band in the United States. One of the bands featured a handsome young soldier named Jackie Fischer, who sang with such style that the young Aussie girls squealed and sighed when they saw him, both on and off the bandstand. He made them forget about Sinatra, Como, Haymes and the rest. I had the privilege of serving as the announcer for the Sunday night broadcasts of the 32nd Division music on 4BC.

Of course, stars from Hollywood were passing through regularly, on their way to entertain in the jungle as part of the USO program. My duties with the band included appearances at military hospitals. This allowed us to entertain those who couldn't get to many of the places where public dances were held. As the war intensified up north, more and more of our personnel spent less time in Brisbane as they were hurried to the battle zones.

It wasn't long before the Armed Forces Radio Service was formed. The unit was charged with building radio stations throughout the world. A Southwest Pacific area office was set up in Brisbane. It was headed by a Hollywood executive, Captain Ted Sherdeman. His job was to assemble teams of military people to establish 50-watt stations in the jungle to entertain and inform our fighting forces in the field.

This was a huge undertaking, with hundreds of people involved from New York to Hollywood. All this work was directed toward broadcasting from a small studio on a secure island in order to inform troops of the war's progress, both in Europe and in the Southwest Pacific area. In addition, these high level radio executives arranged to record all the top radio shows heard regularly in the United States. They then shipped these recordings directly to the stations, where they were played on the air locally. This helped our troops feel closer to home by hearing Jack Benny, Fred Allen, Lux Radio Theater, Fibber McGee and others.

When possible, these programs were played at the same time one would have heard them in the United States. News of the world was heard daily. As a result, building radio stations for our armed forces became a popular project.

On Queen Street in Brisbane one day, I met an old friend, Tommy Allen, a very funny comedian and an enormously talented man. Tommy worked with Special Services and relayed the story of Armed Forces Radio Service (also known as AFRS). At his urging, I visited the office of Ted Sherdeman, who was looking for military people with radio experience to establish stations throughout the Southwest Pacific.

I was surprised to learn that Captain Sherdeman was the same gentleman who at one time had been an executive of KMOX radio back home. After about 30 minutes, he told me to continue in my job, and he would arrange for my transfer into his office. Within five days, I received a notice to report to the AFRS headquarters, just down the street from where I had been working.

After a few more days, Lt. Harmon Nelson, Jr., and I boarded an Air Force C46 for a flight over the Coral Sea to our staging area on the island of Finsch Haven. Before getting a chance to dig in there, we made an evening landing at Port Moresby, New Guinea, where we spent the night. This was the first time I had seen the jungle natives in loin cloths with rings in their noses and ears. They greeted us at the plane and carried the barracks bags to our tent. The natives then ushered us into the mess tent, where we were served some sort of animal meat burned beyond recognition. Dinner also included a new potato, which was raw, and a liquid vegetable, which was hardly appetizing, but a perfect companion to other items on the menu. Some fellows actually tried to eat the meal, but I settled for a candy bar out of a "C" ration kit. Imagine, all this by candlelight in a tent barely sheltering us from the rainy, stormy night. It sounds like something out of a movie script.

The following morning we were up early and ready to reboard our plane for Finsch Haven. No one stopped at the breakfast tent. Our flight was pleasant, and the sun came out, staying with us through our landing midday on Finsch Haven.

After we settled in for some training and work at the radio station on Finsch Haven, we were anxious to get acquainted with our new co-workers and the radio station itself. By this time, we had six or seven enlisted men, who were announcers, along with several technical people. They all were waiting for Lt. Wyn Orr, Capt. Ted Sherdeman and Lt. Nelson to make assignments to the planned stations. None of us had any preference, because all stations would operate uniformly. The concern in my mind was which officer I would get as commander of our unit. Within a few days, I learned I would be going to Los Negros in the Admiralty Islands to build station WVTD. The station manager would be Lt. Harmon Nelson, Jr. I couldn't have been more pleased.

The plan for all stations was to install a commissioned officer to serve as station manager, with the second in command an enlisted man as program director. Remaining personnel would be enlisted people, who would be classified as either announcer/writer or engineer. The officer would be responsible for the entire operation, but the program people were given virtually a free hand to initiate ideas and recruit talent of a local nature.

Hollywood transcribed most network shows, as indicated earlier, and it forwarded these shows to the stations, which would program them without direction from headquarters. But the program director would typically seek out the advice of his station manager to determine the precise day and time of broadcast. We knew our market. We were broadcasting to all troops on the islands, and also to ships at sea which might pick up our signal from the 50-watt transmitter. Among other things, we broadcast news for our people. Because we were aware of the presence of Japanese troops nearby, however, whether on land or sea, we ignored any news which might have helped the enemy. Disc jockey shows started our day at 5 a.m. with a program called "Hit the Deck," which was designed to start off everyone's day. We featured tunes that were popular at home, all played by the big bands of that era.

Our studios were simple but first class. Lt. Nelson worked closely with engineering people to give us a big studio with a piano for live shows. We also had a spacious control room, turntables, a record library, and equipment which allowed us to do remote broadcasts. Our studio shows included music by an orchestra and a military band from the area. We also had talent shows where we afforded singers and other entertainers, both male and female, a chance to be heard on the air. Some were experienced, and others appeared on-air for the first time. We broadcast play-by-play descriptions of a baseball game every Sunday. Although I had covered football and basketball back home, and had successfully auditioned for a professional job, broadcasting baseball was actually a first for me.

Jerry Kauffer, an extremely talented announcer at WGN in Chicago before the war, was on our staff. Jerry possessed one of the most beautiful speaking voices in the world, and he came to us through local recruiting. Then there was Tol Avery. You may not recognize the name, but San Francisco radio audiences knew him very well before the war. He has appeared in dozens of radio, TV shows and movies since his discharge from the Army. George Mataarh was another gifted personality and one of our best disc jockeys.

The Admiralty Islands in the Southwest Pacific area referred mainly to Manus and Los Negros Islands, less than an hour from each other. Manus was a big naval installation and had a "dry dock," which enabled our ships to undergo either simple or extensive repairs without being burdened by lengthy travel. Our radio station was actually located on Los Negros, where all branches of the Armed Forces served, while Manus was primarily a base for the Navy.

But our radio signal reached them all. And from our own personal observations, we were successful. Wherever we went—to the laundry, to the quartermaster, to unit supply, and particularly to the mess halls—we met with compliments and requests for specific music. We even got program ideas from the average soldier and tried to comply with requests in every way. For example, a clerk in the military police offices indicated that he listened to our evening news. He wondered, however, if we could produce a "news in review" program on Sunday night. It was a good idea. And it gave us an opportunity to utilize the talents of a sergeant who was not on our staff, but who had qualifications to do this type of show while remaining in his regular job.

I mentioned our reception by the mess hall personnel. They not only welcomed us but allowed us to eat at unusual hours. They also very often saw to it that we enjoyed goodies that were not on the regular menu.

We were an unusual organization. AFRS was too small to have a records department or mess personnel. We were regarded as other small units were: we were attached to a regular headquarters for "records and rations," which simply meant that we performed our regular duties as necessary, but our personnel files and other records were handled by another organization.

Our lieutenant, Harmon Nelson, actually arranged for our people to eat better than Army personnel usually do. Thanks to Lt. Nelson, the Navy allowed us to eat with them, and the food was outstanding. This was the only military facility I ever visited where a person could specify how he wanted his morning eggs—Scrambled? Over easy? Sunny side up?

With our talented people, our good signal, and the great leadership of Ham Nelson, we felt we operated a station which was well-accepted in the area. The participation of men and women from all services, including Red Cross women who sang with us, added to everyone's enjoyment.

Another plus, of course, was the arrival of USO units—stars from show business who were not in service but who volunteered to leave home and travel halfway around the world to give us word from our native land.

"Stars and Gripes" was a great variety troupe made up of performers who were in the Army but assigned to Special Services. One of these entertainers I got to know rather well. He was Mickey Shaughenessy—whom I later enjoyed when he made many movies and performed on television shows after the war. He was a very funny guy.

Dick Wall announcing at the opening broadcast on WVTD in the Admiralty Islands.

(Left to right) Major Ted Sherdeman, Lieutenant Harmon O. Nelson, Jr., author Dick Wall and announcer George Mataarh outside WVTD.

WVTD opening broadcast.

CHAPTER 26

The Unknown Soldier

Though I spent a very brief period as part of a medical unit, I would never consider myself a qualified "corpsman." The medical training I received was more than an infantry outfit would offer, but at best my time was devoted to "basic training" in medical matters. Nevertheless, one couldn't avoid some of the medical facts made available through literature and on-the-scene observation.

This story is true, but I've chosen to tell it under the above title rather than reveal the soldier's identity. But believe me, it happened.

One of our announcers at an AFRS radio station in the jungle was a highly intelligent college graduate. He had left an excellent job when drafted into the Army. He was also a person who enjoyed discussing many subjects, either in a group or one on one. As a result, he and I spent many hours together in the studio after "sign-off." He was an excellent soldier but, like many of us, wondered why he was there and when he was going home.

He was worried by the presence of a number of Japanese soldiers who were still in the area, although we had been told they were relatively harmless and few in number. Everyone was aware of the occasional "nighttime visit" by Japanese infantrymen. The truth was that these enemy soldiers generally slipped out of their hiding places in a thick tree area on the hill to steal food. They also were sometimes known to pilfer GI laundry, which had been hung out to dry overnight. To our knowledge, they were either unarmed or very lightly armed, and actually happy the war was over, at least for them. But there they were! My friend would panic when he thought of them, showing far more concern than most of us did.

Another thing that disturbed him was the sight and sounds of rats at night. Since rats are nocturnal pests, we really didn't see many during the day. This was a good sign because authorities advise that if you see rats during the daylight hours, they are extremely hungry, or there is such a heavy population of them that they are forced from their nests and are prowling in desperation. But now my friend had this rodent issue to disturb him, though it never affected his work, and our discussions continued. He was a delight and, in fact, drew good-natured jabs about his hang-ups.

One day, my friend told me he had heard that, as the war continued, more and more people were turning themselves in to the hospital, declaring "they couldn't take it any more and wanted to go home." He had heard this was a lucky thing for them, and that some were actually being sent back to the States. He casually mentioned this situation several more times, and I finally tried to set him straight.

"I spent some time at a general hospital, and I can assure you it isn't as easy as you say," I told him. "Someone being sent home, whether with a severe combat wound or a lesser problem, has to be *recommended* for return to the States by a board of doctors. They have to find him unfit for overseas duty. After their decision, he could then be sent back to the States. That's called 'Being Boarded,' and it isn't easy."

As for turning himself in, I reminded him that the Army isn't dumb and that, while I saw some people "sent home" simply for being "unfit for overseas duty," they were first observed by co-workers and commissioned officers to be acting strangely. No one got it done by himself. After several more talks, our discussion periods became less and less frequent, and I really began to pray for this kid, who was becoming more and more withdrawn.

Another one of our announcers noted that my friend had occasionally been late for work and had sometimes failed to return recordings to their jackets after his announcing shift. After checking this out, I decided to talk with this young guy personally, not as a friend but as his program director. He actually expressed regret and said he hadn't realized he had been so inconsiderate. I felt the situation was in hand, so I didn't worry about it. Things proceeded without any special problems, although I felt that at times my ace DJ was, while auditioning records, maintaining an extremely high sound level. He had been asked several times by co-workers to "turn it down."

Over two or three weeks, things seemed under control. But I observed some further changes in my friend. His personal appearance was noticeably not what it had been, despite our generally relaxed approach toward formality in soldierly dress. Most perplexing was the gleam of amazement he displayed when talking about music. He appeared to be developing an unusual fixation on the subject, one which bordered on the obsessive. And his eyes opened wide when he explained the renewed enthusiasm for his job. He was good at his work, but I continued to worry about him.

My concern turned to pity when I walked into our record library one afternoon to find the person who had become my biggest problem sitting on the floor in the center of the room, literally knee deep in recordings and transcriptions. Some 300 discs had been taken from the alphabetized files and scattered around the room. When he saw me, those eyes widened again, and he said he was anxious to install a new filing system. For the first time, I departed from my usually relaxed style and laid down the law. With only the two of us present, I felt it was my chance to explain in no uncertain terms what we needed in our radio station, and what I needed from him. I left the room noting that all of us on staff would have to help restore our library to a workable state.

While I had not discussed any of these incidents with our commanding officer, he asked me if I had noticed anything unusual about our man. I thought this might be my chance to open up a little. Because until this moment, the whole thing had been my responsibility. Slowly, as we talked, many of the situations which had seemed unrelated now took on a more ominous character. I soon placed the whole picture before our leader, and it felt better to share the load with him. Since the recently promoted Major Sherdeman was going to pay us a visit shortly, the officer and I agreed to talk with him and get his thinking on the situation, to see whether or not we had a truly serious problem. Meanwhile, my friend continued to work, performing flawlessly. But his wide eyes and the loud music continued.

When the top brass arrived to look over our operation, my biggest problem, of course, came up. After three days, the strange behavior of our most talented colleague was strongly evident. It was unanimous—we agreed to send our boy to the hospital for examination. He seemed surprised to hear the decision, but since the medical group was on our island, it didn't seem to be such a big deal. Without any fanfare, one of our people drove him to the medical center, and our announcer checked into the hospital.

For several days, we visited our friend. We dedicated music and even entire programs to him. We took our equipment to the hospital to do a "remote" from the rec room where, for the first time, we allowed a patient to conduct the show. Then our commanding officer got word through the grapevine that our favorite patient was going to appear before the board of doctors who would decide his fate. And so we waited. After several days, the word came down:

he was being sent back to the United States for disposition. Reason: "Unfit for overseas duty."

I have to admit that I heard the news with mixed emotions. I was happy to see him get to go home, but I regretted seeing him possibly headed for a psychiatric discharge, more commonly known as a "Section 8."

It was almost standard operating procedure (at least where we were) that persons "boarded" remain in the hospital until air or ship transportation became available. On the day of departure, they were literally tagged with a shipping label attached to the robe or shirt and told to wait for the bus taking them to the point of embarkation. Because of his popularity, our man was allowed to visit the station one last time, just before he departed. The hour he spent with us was bright, and a virtual celebration atmosphere prevailed. He was a great talent.

Just as our hour was about to end, the guest of honor called me aside to shake hands and to say so long. Suddenly the wide eyes vanished, and a sudden seriousness came over him, the likes of which I hadn't seen for many weeks.

He broke into a gentle smile and quickly squeezed my hand. I had the feeling I was saying good-bye to an old friend. Perhaps, I thought, to the same untarnished soldier with whom I had so many late night talk sessions not too long ago.

My suspicions were confirmed when he said softly, "Thanks for everything. I couldn't have done it without you. You were so right, the Army isn't dumb. I couldn't have done it alone. Thanks, good friend, the bus is about to leave. I'll write when I get home."

Only then did I realize I'd been had. All of the things I had prescribed for the person who wanted to go home were slowly woven into a neat picture. Separately the pieces meant nothing. The mosaic, however, spelled h-o-m-e.

A few weeks later, I received a letter from my friend. It was on the letterhead of a major commercial radio station, where he was working as a featured personality in the United States. He's still a star—and he's still my friend.

CHAPTER 27

Bob Hope

It is a fact of life that some persons live comfortably with success, while others become so full of themselves when fortune smiles that they just can't handle it.

Strangely enough, where the latter type is concerned, they often are ideal individuals in the entertainment business. But put them in a position of authority in the military, and they just go wild. An example that comes to mind is a giant singing star of the '30s and '40s. He had the world at his feet when he sang in radio, movies and nightclubs. After starring on the old *Hit Parade*, he left radio to become an ensign in the wartime Navy.

Lt. Harmon "Ham" Nelson was one of those people who made the switch from show business to service with ease. My family had sent me clippings from the St. Louis papers noting that Nelson had left Hollywood to enter the Army. Some pointed out that many USO stars had seen him and reported on how they had visited him in the jungle. I had found that, while "Ham" was never one to brag, his most casual conversation indicated that he numbered among his prewar friends many Hollywood stars. And, of course, his marriage to film star Bette Davis was further proof. Nevertheless, his charm, personality and great musical talent were such that he had little or no trouble making friends at all levels.

Our unit had been aware that Bob Hope and his troupe of entertainers were going to visit the islands. But no specific dates had been announced. When notified that they had landed, the recently promoted Captain Nelson and I went over to Manus to arrange for broadcast of the program on WVTD. We had plans to meet the famous comedian briefly, just to lay the groundwork for our broadcast. We were all business.

As we walked along the Manus Company Street, Captain Nelson and I were virtually unnoticed by the people we passed—with one big exception! One of the loudest and most recognized voices in the world came booming from the mouth of Jerry Colonna, the big band trombonist who had become a radio and movie comedy star when he joined the Bob Hope group. His stentorian voice let most of the island know that Nelson was there, as he shouted in that Colonna style, "Ham, you son of a gun, wait for me!" He ran down the street, to where we had stopped, and embraced Nelson like a long lost brother. They were old friends.

Jerry directed us to Hope's quarters, promising to catch up with us later. The mustachioed, saucer-eyed star was genuinely excited, and he obviously assumed we would have no trouble seeing Hope.

Then it began! The runaround developed as we approached the officer (the "singing ensign" mentioned above), who was responsible for Bob's security. This officer didn't recognize "Ham" as he shuffled papers and vocalized the standard, "You can't just walk in here and see Bob Hope. Everybody wants to see him. He's resting. And when he gets up, he has to do a show. I'm sorry, you can't see Mr. Hope today." His arrogance was suffocating.

Ham remained calm and made two additional efforts to convince the ensign that seeing Bob Hope was important, but he finally agreed to respect the ensign's wishes. I asked "Ham" if he had told him who he was, but he insisted that he didn't operate that way. So we sat and waited.

As the singer went about his "duties," he pointedly ignored us until Jerry Colonna came into the reception room. Jerry rushed up to Ham, and they hugged again. Jerry asked why we were still waiting to see Hope. Nelson, still unwilling to blame the ensign, just shrugged, stating we would have to wait until Hope woke up.

Colonna was furious, but always a gentleman. He escorted us past the reception desk—some 50 feet—into Bob Hope's room. As Hope saw us, he was sitting on a bed massaging his feet; tired from overwork, including the dancing in his act. After Ham introduced me to Hope and engaged in the usual small talk, the four of us chatted and discussed plans for the show for nearly 45 minutes, after which we left to arrange for our broadcast.

As a former network producer, Nelson sized up the facilities and made several suggestions designed to improve not only broadcast conditions but the entire Bob Hope show.

The moral of our story? Although Hope and Colonna were aware of the pettiness of the ensign's action, they were big enough not to make an issue of it. Nothing was said, but the ensign realized how foolish he looked. As we left he said nothing, though his embarrassment was evident.

It's easy to recognize a truly capable officer like Harmon O. Nelson, Jr., who could adjust to any situation, professional or social. And then there's that other fellow, the insufferable Ensign So-and-So. I know his name, but I'm trying to forget it.

CHAPTER 28

Return to Paradise

After many months in the islands, which had been secured by marines, air force and infantry, I was notified that
in view of my time overseas, I had a good prospect of going home soon. The "point system," a program devised in
Washington to determine the order in which our people
would return to the States, indicated that I was soon to be
shipped home. I had heard that my original outfit, the 105th
General Hospital with whom I had come overseas, was now
operating a hospital on the island of Biak, where we had a
sister station, WVTG. I had so many friends there: John
Viducich, Jim Cavanaugh, Von Wilbur and others, many
from St. Louis. I thought I would like to see them again. So

I asked that I be assigned to WVTG. Approval was prompt, but I waited a couple of days for transportation. Although there were aircraft going to Biak daily, I didn't have top priority. Persons whose visits there were more important got the first call, and rightly so.

I arrived at my destination on a cloudy morning and was met by Lt. Matt Lynch. He was the station manager and a good man, but he lacked broadcast experience, and thus had no idea of how to operate a radio station. I had heard of this situation and felt somewhat relieved when I found that two enlisted men, Randy English and Chuck Hotteling, had stepped in. With experience gained before the war, they had been able to keep the ship afloat.

Things were rolling along because the format was almost identical to WVTD, with music, news, American-transcribed shows and local sports. It would be difficult for anyone to fail with it.

I registered with the local military people, who were setting up a staging area for people being "rotated back to the states." On a first-come basis, we were placed on a list of persons slated to return home. Without regard to rank, we shipped out on the first transportation available.

I was allowed to work and live at headquarters while waiting. The first sergeant at the rotation camp assured me that, if I called him each morning, he could let me know whether my name was posted among those boarding for the U.S. that day. I could thus report in and, if not scheduled for departure, could continue to work at the station that day.

The inevitable came one morning when I called my contact at the rotation center. I was told to proceed without delay for processing and quick boarding of the USS *Anderson*, which was sailing on that day. Everyone in AFRS was quick to help me get ready. They drove me to the dock. That night, along with hundreds of other vets, I was steaming toward the USA. Included on our passenger list was a group of Americans who had been held captive by the Japanese. They had been freed only a few days before and were headed home.

To say that the hundreds of American officers, nurses and enlisted men enjoyed an uneventful trip is, of course, an understatement. But it seemed that, as excited as we all were, each of us tried to appear cool, as if this were just another boat ride. But we were all thrilled. Because many of us slept on deck at night, I knew it was possible to detect a smile on the faces of many, even while they were sleeping, particularly those who had been prisoners of the Japanese. They were such special people. It must have seemed strange to them that, while they were heroic and long-suffering enlisted men crowded into our section, they saw officers and nurses, some who had never heard a shot fired in anger, quartered topside in greater comfort. Yet these brave people never complained. For two weeks we all ate, slept and, I'm sure, dreamed of home. Then it appeared on the horizon: San Francisco! Because this group of prisoners was the first to return home, a huge welcome was planned. Naturally, those of us who could never imagine the suffering our prisoner brothers had experienced were more than willing to understand who the welcome was really for. We arrived in the San Francisco area the night before we were due to disembark, and the *Anderson* anchored a short distance from the harbor until morning.

I've never seen such a welcome. When we began our movement toward land, boats and ships of all sizes flew that beautiful American flag. Bands played, cannon salutes sounded, and dignitaries aboard many of the vessels joined in the welcome. Mrs. Franklin D. Roosevelt, the First Lady of our land, was on hand to let our people know they were welcomed home.

After a couple of hours in celebration, we landed on American soil. While our real heroes were delayed long enough to receive personal welcomes, the remainder of us made our way to troop trains for our ride back to the Midwest. We were home!

Although most of us tried to keep our feelings of excitement and anticipation under control while heading home, I couldn't help but wonder if others gave as much thought as I did to the hundreds of USO performers who gave of their time and energy to entertain us while overseas.

They were persons who, because of age or perhaps a physical limitation, were not accepted in the services, even though many of them had volunteered. Yet they were ready and anxious to help our cause in any way they could. Not only were these talented persons seen at bond rallies and "canteens," but many entertained deep in the jungle, where the war was thick and where the dangers occasioned by bullets and other explosives weren't limited to military personnel.

In addition to entertaining the troops, many of them saw to it that they mingled with our men and women, often taking down phone numbers of relatives in the States and carrying messages to those waiting at home.

From Bob Hope and Jack Benny to some of the lesser knowns, these performers were at their best, regardless of audience size, from several hundred to 10,000. Our troops deserved it—and they received it.

CHAPTER 29

Headin' Home

It may be that all troop trains are pretty much the same. But every soldier traveling home has his own unique story.

We boarded about noon on the day of our arrival from overseas. After four restless hours, I heard and felt the wheels of the St. Louis-bound locomotive easing out of the San Francisco station, with cars of service people bringing up the rear.

Unlike the average train, which residents of small towns and larger cities might have seen crossing the country, this one was packed with war-tired men and women. It made frequent stops, where the locals would actually greet and shake hands with the passengers.

Troops were really given a chance to stretch their legs—and to visit a store or hamburger stand in many towns, where their railroad to home waited a maximum of 15 minutes before chugging out again. Obviously, the stops were planned, and they really served as a chance for returnees to ease into a new lifestyle. Despite the desire of most to get home as soon as possible, the stops were appreciated.

The only persons who sincerely frowned upon the stops, as I saw it, were the big winners in blackjack and crap games, which made the three-day train ride seem shorter. The old story goes, "The winners tell jokes, and the losers say 'deal.' " But as I recall in this case, the winners were anxious to continue to "deal."

Some of the passengers used the brief stops to place phone calls home. Remember, we went directly from the *Anderson* to our train, and only a few had been able to find an available telephone. I had written from the jungle to let my family know that I was being rotated to the States, but no dates were specified. So when we stopped in a small Colorado town (I never knew its name), I managed to notify my folks that I would be home in two days.

On our train, we were advised that, upon reaching St. Louis, we would all be transported by bus to Jefferson Barracks, on the south side of St. Louis, for processing before reassignment. Now my mind was centered on home.

We arrived at Union Station in St. Louis on March 16, 1945, at about 10:30 p.m. Those in charge told us to depart through a station exit on Market Street in order to board the bus for Jefferson Barracks.

Although there were several hundred of us heading to the barracks, only a small number were from St. Louis and thus needed a phone. It was almost 11 p.m. when I dialed that familiar number. My dad answered, and I greeted him as though this were just a routine call and I had never been away. That didn't last long. Although my dad was not an emotional man, I nevertheless thought I detected a tear in his voice when he realized who was calling.

I talked to him and to my mom only briefly, because I didn't want to miss the bus. So I told them I'd call the next day. I tossed and turned a lot that night. Like a little child, I could hardly wait for morning.

CHAPTER 30

Jefferson Barracks

I had three projects for March 17, 1945, my first day home in more than three years. First, I wanted to get my processing out of the way. Second, I wanted to explore the possibility of an assignment to Special Services in St. Louis. Third, I was eager to see my family after so many years away.

I approached the front desk of the Jefferson Barracks Reception Center headquarters to inquire about their personnel situation. I explained the details of my jobs overseas, stressing my entertainment experience. The private at that desk told me he was to be discharged within the next month and that there would be an opening for a Special Services corporal in that office. He generously volunteered that, despite the background I had described, "The sergeant who is our ranking enlisted man is an entertainer, a pianist-singer and MC, so we don't need your background. We need someone with athletic experience. When you talk to the lieutenant, push the sports side."

I was ushered into the office of WAC Lieutenant Heideman, who was responsible for staffing the administrative offices of the Reception Center. I explained my overseas service, that my home was St. Louis, and that I hoped I could spend the rest of my service locally. I didn't lie to her, but I did hit heavily on my athletic knowledge, and that I could be of help in any other area where she needed a backup.

She introduced me to her noncom, Jack Breen, who was a talented pianist, singer and well-known entertainer in St. Louis. Both Jack and the lieutenant seemed pleased with our meeting, but they were noncommittal regarding my assignment. So I resumed processing after leaving my name, rank and serial number with everyone who would listen.

Because the Army didn't want to disturb the 30-day annual furlough plan, a "Delay Enroute" system was put into use. Anyone who returned from overseas on rotation was ordered to Hot Springs, Arkansas, for reassignment. So that everyone would be able to have some time at home, however, the orders called for a "Delay Enroute," which would give a person perhaps two weeks in which to get to Hot Springs. This procedure gave each person two weeks at home without having to use furlough time.

I received my travel orders that first day at Jefferson Barracks and spent the evening at 4512 Chouteau with my mom and dad, and with sister Doris and her husband, Bill Hagerty. The next 14 days allowed me to see old buddies who were not in service and to date some old friends from pre-1942. And, oh yes, to sip some "Bud" in old haunts like "Candlelight," the "Walnut Room" and the Chase and Park Plaza.

The Delay Enroute came to an end, and a report to the Arlington Hotel in Hot Springs was in order. This hotel had been taken over by the Army and converted into a resort spot. After our trips home, several hundred other GIs and I registered as guests. Three wonderful meals, an orchestra playing during lunch and dinner, the famous baths, tickets to the track and other events, and all of this provided free. Many engaged couples waited for the order to Arlington before taking that walk down the aisle.

The buck sergeant in charge of Special Services at the Arlington was Dennis James, who had worked on the networks as a radio announcer. To this day, he is still seen on TV across the nation.

The week of high living was interrupted from time to time in order to allow some of the group to speculate concerning where we would be assigned next. When I mentioned that I had bid for a Special Services spot in my hometown of St. Louis but didn't know exactly where I would end up, the standard GI comment came from most of my group: "I never asked the Army for anything, and I ain't starting now!"

On Friday afternoon, the assignments were published. People went to Cheyenne, Wyoming; Fort Hood, Texas; and

Fort Dix, New Jersey. And on that list of assignments was "Dick Wall to Special Services, Reception Center, Jefferson Barracks, St. Louis, Missouri!"

I was happy to get my orders to report to Jefferson Barracks. They came, oddly enough, on Friday, April 13, 1945. My new assignment helped lift the gloom that settled in after some bad news 24 hours earlier. On the 12th, I had been waiting for my orders, not patiently, when a radio voice boomed through the lobby with an announcement that President Franklin D. Roosevelt had died. Although he had been in poor health for a long time, his death came as a tremendous shock.

The radio details could be heard throughout the lobby, as everyone within hearing distance stopped in his tracks. The disbelief on many faces soon turned to tears. The remainder of the afternoon and evening saw cancellation of events originally planned to buoy the spirits of returning soldiers, who now had lost their Commander-in-Chief and the only President many could remember. Instead, everyone seemed inclined toward just sitting and talking to others who were equally dumbfounded.

I have to admit that some of the pleasures of anticipating a new assignment were dampened a little that day.

By the following Monday, however, I was into my new job. The duties weren't limited. They included everything from purchasing and issuing athletic equipment, organizing baseball leagues, supervising maintenance of athletic fields, to handling the paging of new recruits who had visitors on post. These duties were shared by all of us in the office. It appeared I would be here until my separation from the Army.

CHAPTER 31

St. Louis Duty

I guess every soldier from St. Louis gave at least some thought to how nice it would be to find himself assigned permanently to Jefferson Barracks. I know I had that dream when I was drafted. But after shipping out to basic training less than a week from induction, it soon faded. The second time around was different. Not only was I very pleased to have the Jefferson Barracks assignment, I was surprised to learn that some of the "permanent party" had been there throughout the war.

For most of us, the duties were routine, but the freedom was new. Each of us was assigned a bunk on post, which we had to keep orderly. The bed had to be made when we weren't using it, and the area to which we were assigned was to be "GI." The bright spot was that we were issued "Class A" passes and were allowed to sleep away from the company quarters, so long as we attended certain formations and kept out of trouble.

As a result, doing the kind of work I enjoyed, plus being able to live with my parents while serving in the Army, was quite an enviable position. It was certainly an improvement over living in the jungles of New Guinea.

For me, it became a regimen of ordering athletic equipment, organizing and scheduling sporting events, making war bond speeches to St. Louis area groups and, of course, manning the microphone several nights each week during visiting hours. We were off on weekends, so putting in a few extra hours occasionally wasn't too difficult to endure. In fact, responding to questions from civilian visitors resulted in what was, without a doubt, the most important discovery of my life.

CHAPTER 32

Buddy Is Drafted

One can understand that every mother, father, wife or other family member was anxious to see the young rookie who had left the family home to become a soldier. To view him for the first time, fresh from saddle oxfords, button-down shirt and sport coat, and strutting in his new (though not necessarily well-fitted) GI uniform, was a source of great pride and some anxiety to family members.

And there were all types of visitors. Being unfamiliar with the Army and Army methods, they approached me, a corporal, with uncertainty. As I manned the microphone and paged soldier after soldier, some felt they would get a quicker response from their new GI if they spoke to me softly and politely. Others addressed me with an authoritative tone, telling me of the family members who were in Congress or who knew people in high places. Many brought "bribes" of soda pop, homemade cookies, and so on. In truth, however, those of us who did the paging had no power at all. If the new men were free and available, they would report to our meeting room. But occasionally they were momentarily delayed, which would cause anxiety among the relatives for some 15 or 20 minutes.

The most memorable of all visitors occurred while I was on duty June 7, 1945. It seems that a young man from Richmond Heights, Missouri, a suburb of St. Louis, had one day earlier been drafted and was processing at our reception center. He was visited that evening by his parents, Leo and Ellen Bub, and four sisters (Mary Ellen, Alice, Theresa and Betty) as well as a brother, Bill. Now this family was anxious to see "Buddy," but they were also upset when he didn't respond to the first two pages. One by one, Mom and Dad, and then the four sisters approached me with big smiles, Coca-Cola and cookies. But the sisters' smiles soon turned to ice as I repeatedly told them "Buddy" was not yet available. (I had now begun to page "Buddy" Bub instead of Private Leo Bub. Although I had never even seen the lad, I began to feel like I was one of the family.) One of the young ladies then came up with a new approach.

The young lady said, "My name is Teedy, and Buddy is my twin brother, and we have just *got* to see him."

She made some sarcastic reference to what an easy job I had sitting there talking into the microphone all evening. She also wondered how I ever obtained such soft duty. Finally the four sisters huddled around my desk, and I noticed they were a particularly attractive family. Billy, who seemed to be about ten, didn't comment at all, but he was there to back up the Bub gang.

Bear in mind, all of this was going on while more visitors were arriving and more soldiers were responding. In desperation, I finally took the mike in hand and made a special announcement.

"Ladies and gentlemen, your attention please." It seemed that everyone in the area, hundreds of visitors and scores of recruits, stopped and stood at attention. After all, the country was at war, and they were on a military base. I continued my announcement:

"Stop the War! Stop the War! Four young ladies at the information desk are trying to locate a member of their family. It seems that Buddy Bub—he is the twin of Teedy here—has not answered his page. Please be on the lookout for Private Bub and tell him his twin is waiting for him and that it is urgent."

In about five minutes, Leo Bub, Jr., showed up and all was well. Mother, father, the four sisters, and Bill thanked me, and normal life was restored. But the father still felt that cookies and Coca-Cola had produced the results. Now I mention this only because I said I had gotten to feel like a member of that family. I later phoned Mary Ellen, the oldest and the quiet one, and asked her for a date.

One year later, on June 15, 1946, Mary Ellen and I walked down the aisle of St. Luke's the Evangelist Catholic Church in Richmond Heights. She has given me three wonderful sons and a great set of in-laws.

I have often wondered if her father ever regretted investing in Coca-Cola and chocolate chip cookies.

I must mention that each member of the family has done very well. Alice completed her career as executive secretary to the board chairman of a major St. Louis bank. Betty and her husband, Chick Hirt, reared four wonderful children (Mary Elizabeth, Barbara, Charles and Joe) before Betty's death in 1983. Theresa Rose, the Teedy in our story, joined a religious order, the Sisters of Saint Joseph of Carondelet. For many years, Sister Leo Ann served as Mother Superior and principal of Saint Roch's Convent and School at Rosedale and Waterman in St. Louis. Today, as she observes her Golden Jubilee celebrating 50 years in the convent, Sister Leo Ann continues to serve God and His people by working at a skilled nursing home in Shrewsbury, Missouri. Her twin, Buddy, and his wife Shirley reared five children (Leo III, Sarah, Chris, Mike and David). Buddy recently retired from a distinguished 40-year career at Dow Chemical. Young Bill and his late wife, Ann, reared two children (Brigid and Bill, Jr.). After a stint in the U.S. Navy and a career in the building materials industry, Bill later followed his brother, Buddy, to Dow, where they shared an office suite.

CHAPTER 33

A Soldier's Story

This part of the book, with my World War II reminiscences, would be incomplete without a special chapter on Ray Steitz, the best wartime buddy a soldier could have.

Ray was that rare individual who could do it all. He was an outstanding athlete at Christian Brothers College High School in St. Louis. Ray achieved even greater success at the collegiate level, where he starred as captain of the varsity basketball team at St. Louis University. Combining his tremendous athletic ability with a brilliant intellect and social grace, Ray could have been a great success in any field he chose, including professional basketball or baseball. Ray decided to pursue law, however, and he graduated from the St. Louis University School of Law shortly before his induction into the Army.

I had known Ray through my sports reporting in St. Louis, of course, but I had also enjoyed seeing him socially during those tranquil years before the war. I really got to know Ray well, however, only after both of us entered the military. Ray and I ended up in the same outfit and were assigned for basic training together at Fort Lewis. How well I remember that train ride from St. Louis to Seattle! Ray served up food on the chow line during our trip. Imagine, a lawyer ladling out rolled oats to the troops! You can be certain that Ray filled our mess kits to the brim—and made a friend of everyone on the train.

Upon reaching Fort Lewis, we were assigned to the same barracks, with Ray in the lower bunk and me in the upper deck. After our basic training began, more than 300 GIs quickly learned to appreciate Ray's friendly grin and kind words, which made being away from home a bit easier to endure. Ray was truly a joy to be around, and we became the best of friends.

It didn't take long for the Army to notice what enlisted men had known all along—Ray's talents and abilities fit him to serve as an officer. He was quickly selected for Officer Candidate School. Within 90 days, Ray graduated from OCS with highest honors and was promoted to second lieutenant.

His first assignment was as a platoon leader in some of the bloodiest hand-to-hand fighting in New Guinea. As in everything he undertook, Ray distinguished himself in combat as well. We corresponded regularly and, when Ray

*Dick Wall (tallest man, in center) with Ray Steitz
(immediately behind) in mess line.*

had leave, he returned to Brisbane, where our outfit was stationed at the time.

During one of those leaves, Ray confided to me over a couple of cold Budweisers what he considered to be the toughest part of his job as a combat officer. It wasn't the personal danger. It wasn't the primitive living conditions. It was sending men on patrols from which some of them would never return.

"Dick, we'd all like to be officers," Ray said. "But it's not all glamour. The hardest thing I've ever had to do is to sit in the jungle, surrounded by Japanese soldiers, and send young men to scout for enemy troops with the knowledge that odds were against some of them ever to return. No man should be asked to send people into that kind of a situation. But that's the price one pays for a commission."

Ray and I continued to be close after the war, enjoying sports, double dating, and the thousand and one other things that good friends share. Ray was even the best man at my wedding.

Ray Steitz went on to enjoy a brilliant career as an insurance executive and as an adjunct professor, teaching law to future generations of young people in St. Louis. At his untimely death almost twenty years ago, Ray left a beautiful wife, Kathleen, six loving children (Ray, Jim, Patricia, Mary, John and Tom), and countless friends, all of whom are better for having known and loved him.

Ray Steitz (left) and Dick Wall (in jeep) at Fort Lewis, Washington.

CHAPTER 34

An End to War

With the war over in Europe and the surrender of Japan imminent, those of us who remained in service began to look toward discharge day. October 1, 1945, was the day they handed me papers which authorized my going where I wanted, wearing the clothes of my choice. Shortly before my official discharge date, the Army told me that I was free to go back to WTMV to handle the play-by-play of East St. Louis High School football games on Friday nights. This was, of course, on my own time. So, instead of drawing the federal grant of $20 each week for 52 weeks, which was available to unemployed war veterans (more commonly known as the "52-20 Club"), I went to work full time at

WTMV just five days before my official departure from the Army.

The excitement of daily activities in the studios was even greater than I thought it would be. Though we operated on only 250 watts, we had programming and production professionalism comparable to many of the more powerful stations in the St. Louis market. Our studios were still in the Broadview Hotel in East St. Louis, under the guidance of general manager Mike Henry.

Paul Enright, our program director, rode herd on a talented announcing staff. We all had a chance to do what we liked to do and, for the most part, what we did best. Bill Hart was still at the piano and serving as music director. Live musical shows were broadcast daily, as were my "Man on the Street" shows from 7th and Washington in downtown St. Louis, and our hourly news shows. Bob Terry was as smooth an announcer as any station had.

Broadcasting from the Broadview meant that we had an almost steady flow of people who just wanted to look in on a live radio show, although all of us were quite surprised to have visitors ask for autographs.

Athletes and sports promoters were frequent guests at the station. This included everyone from Harry Caray, who for a long time broadcast a daily sports show on WTMV, to such baseball stars as Rogers Hornsby, Grover Cleveland Alexander, Stan Musial, Johnnie Sturm and others.

CHAPTER 35

What a Guy

Working as the master of ceremonies can be a wonderful experience, particularly when you work with well-known entertainers, and especially when you're only 25 years old. For several years at WTMV, I had done MC work, "Man on the Street" shows and conducted interviews with political figures, but this was nothing compared to the experience gained in Armed Forces Radio Service and in Base Section Three Special Services.

The excitement of meeting and introducing such people as John Wayne, Bob Hope, Mickey Shaughenessy, Ray Bolger, Artie Shaw and others is more than a lowly corporal had any reason to expect. With isolated exceptions,

I never knew any of them so well that they would call me after the war. But it happened!

After the war, I was back in St. Louis wearing civilian clothes when I received a phone call from Ray Bolger—the same man who had played the "Scarecrow" in that great movie *Wizard of Oz*. Ray called just to see how I was doing. I would have thought someone was putting me on had the caller not referred to times I had introduced him and pianist Little Jack Little in Australia. His familiarity with me and with the things we had talked about was indeed gratifying.

I am convinced that he had kept some kind of diary on his USO trips and actually called many of us. And he did this just because he cared. One thing I know—Ray Bolger, the singer who made the top recording of "Once in Love with Amy," increased his popularity among so many of us who knew and worked with him ever so briefly, just because he was such a great guy.

CHAPTER 36

A Search for Sales

Someone once said that the worst day of work in a radio performer's life is far more enjoyable than the best day for a person in any other line of work. I am inclined to agree with that. But radio also includes sales management and the executive life, and sales intrigued me.

We had a crack sales team at WTMV. It was made up of veteran people, which left little chance of an opening. Out-of-town stations seemed at that time to prefer local people in sales, and combination announcer/sales positions were unusual.

So I let it be known throughout the St. Louis radio industry that I was interested in sales, but no one was knocking down my door. I also thought public relations was an area where my experience would fit quite well.

In any event, I began to think about sales during the first year or two after my discharge from the Army.

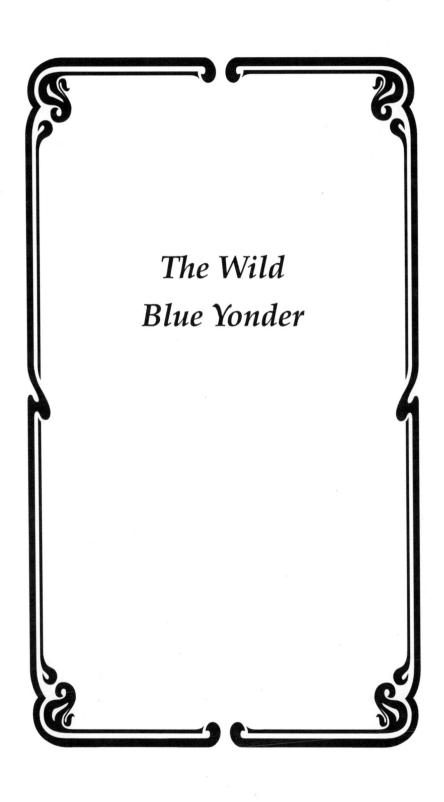

The Wild
Blue Yonder

CHAPTER 37

Mr. Mac

As I look back on the many wonderful associations I have enjoyed in life, I find it difficult to rank one over another. My great enthusiasm for the broadcast side of radio never dampened, but a desire to be in sales and management gradually developed. And it soon occurred to me that making the move from production to sales was going to be difficult, if not impossible, unless someone would gamble on me. It had been suggested that I go into public relations. At that time, however, most people really had little information on the field of public relations. Many felt it was the art of "meeting people" and being a "glad-hander." It is obviously much more than that. In most cases, it calls for all of the above, plus an ability to write and to have some insight into the business sector. The fact was that no radio station I knew employed people in a purely public relations role, so prospects were dim.

At a social gathering, I was introduced to a McDonnell Aircraft Corporation executive who seemed interested in discussing St. Louis radio. He was fascinated by the whole business and appeared puzzled that I would consider getting out of it. He gave me the name of a person to contact if I became serious about making a change. In a few weeks, I called Mr. Duke Windsor at MAC and asked for an appointment.

Of course, I knew I had no qualifications for sales in the aircraft field. But Duke offered me a position in McDonnell's personnel department, where he was the

Dick Wall as an employment interviewer at MAC.

Dick Wall during his years at McDonnell Aircraft.

employment manager. As an interviewer, I would be meeting people who were seeking a job. I decided to accept the offer. The basic position was "screener," which entailed talking to persons who had completed an application. I would then refer those with even basic skills to a more experienced interviewer, who would talk to the applicant in more detail.

During slow days, senior interviewers Gerry Whittington and Bud O'Toole worked closely with me. I was encouraged to visit various departments, such as machine shops and assembly areas, where I could better familiarize myself with the needs of each supervisor. After a few months, I moved into my own office and had authority to make my own hires. Gerry, Bud and Duke Windsor, however, were always available for advice and suggestions.

Eventually, I traveled to college campuses in an effort to recruit senior class engineering students. I was authorized to set salaries and extend offers of employment. During all of the next two years, I found an atmosphere of joy and friendship unexcelled anywhere.

McDonnell employees were what the corporation's founder, James McDonnell, wanted them to be—a team. An employee association was headed by my old friend, Bert Granville, the same person who had starred as a singer and MC in radio and nightclubs. Through his work at McDonnell, Bert brought all of us closer with dances, theatrical productions and an annual picnic. Through the employee association, the company made baseball, softball and all other sports available. If an employee wanted to participate in an activity, he or she needed only to ask, and a program would be developed. As I recall, we even had a chess tournament.

When they make a list of great places to work, MAC will certainly be among the leaders. But even though I felt there were opportunities for moving up in the future, I was content with my duties and associates, and I imagined that I would be there for a long time. Though I was allowed by management to free-lance in radio, I was on the MAC team.

A Bud
for Everyone

Gussie Busch

I don't profess to have an unusual insight into the Anheuser or Busch families or their business. But this book is about a beer drummer, so comments about the families or the empire will be supplied as necessary for the story.

In view of the fact that the history of the Anheuser-Busch families is so detailed that one writer took more than a thousand pages to relate the story, it is not necessary to go into that here. However, information on August A. Busch, Jr., who was at the top during the period of my association with the brewery, is imperative, because he made the brewery go!

August A. Busch, Jr., was in his 50s when I first met him. A heavyset, athletic type, his rugged, deeply-lined face and thinning hair topped a roly-poly body, which really reminded one of a true Beer Baron. But his gruff voice was one thing you would never forget. Anything but a mean man, he was a friend to all who worked for him, yet one felt certain he was the type of person you would never want for an enemy. He was concerned for everyone: his employees, their families, the working man and woman, and the general public. Stories of his generosity echoed not only throughout the brewery, but across the streets of St. Louis and beyond.

For example, a friend once told me of working as a volunteer with a group which assumed responsibility for raising $20,000 to assure existence of the St. Louis Symphony Orchestra. He said he didn't know where to start and, without family background or social position, he was reluctant to knock on the doors of prominent civic leaders, feeling they would not respond to him.

But he had heard of Mr. Busch's down-to-earth attitude and went to call on him. After getting in to the executive's office, he explained his position. He said he had to raise $20,000 but felt it would be a long, difficult task. He told Mr. Busch, "If you would start with $5,000, Mr. Busch, other business leaders might be inclined to follow, and we could whip this thing."

Mr. Busch, I'm told, listened for a few minutes, ordered two phone calls to check the man out, and then called in an assistant and told her, "Get a check to this man for $20,000. The symphony orchestra can't wait."

Another story deals with an accident that occurred in the New Jersey brewery early in the '50s. Several Anheuser-Busch employees were injured. Shortly after news of the tragedy reached the St. Louis office, a meeting was called where the questions of employee insurance and family benefits were discussed by top executives and company lawyers.

The story goes that, in typical August Busch fashion, he brought the gathering to a close by directing an aide to "Forget about the forms that have to be filled out and who is entitled to what. Get to every family affected by this thing and see that they have enough cash in their hands to carry them through this disaster. See that they have the money today, and we'll worry about the damn paperwork later."

Mr. Busch was also an avid sportsman. Across the country, he is perhaps best remembered today as the owner of our St. Louis Cardinals baseball team. After purchasing the club in 1953, he had championship teams, and then some others that had local fans almost in tears. But all clubs were instilled with the championship attitude of Mr. Busch. He always had an insatiable desire to win. Anything short of victory was unacceptable. So he had several managers and made many trades. One thing Mr. Busch and the St. Louis fans always felt was that there was a championship in the Cardinals' future. He wouldn't have had it any other way.

Mr. Busch was always a great animal lover and sportsman. Grant's Farm in suburban St. Louis, the family home, covers more than 280 acres, and the 34-room mansion is surrounded by a beautiful wooded area, sheltering hundreds of animals and birds. They are not only enjoyed by

Dick Wall (standing second from left) with Gussie Busch (seated second from left) and A. B. Anheuser (standing third from right) entertaining a group of retailers at Grant's Farm.

the generous Busch family, but are viewed by several hundred thousand visitors every year.

Mr. Busch, a nationally known sportsman and breeder of Clydesdale horses, took extreme pleasure in entertaining kings and peasants alike at his estate. The only requirement was that they be sports and animal lovers. August A. Busch, Jr. was truly a high class gentleman with the common touch.

I often worked with Mr. Busch, attended meetings in his office, and went to parties at the fabulous Grant's Farm home. (Named, incidentally, because the farm was once worked by General U. S. Grant. A cabin the General occupied is still located there.) But I, along with many others who knew and respected him, always referred to him as

Mr. Busch. Yet I never met a person in a bar, restaurant or sports event, most of whom had never even seen him, who didn't chummily call him "Gussie." This never bothered him. All he wanted was for the world to be kind to animals, to root for the Cardinals, and to drink Budweiser, Busch or Michelob beer (not necessarily in that order).

He truly felt there were only two kinds of beer in the world. Those made by Anheuser-Busch— and root beer. In fact, his number one competitor at that time was never mentioned by name, either in the brewery offices or at the farm. "Schultz" was the closest we ever came to the correct name.

Some of the stories about him may be legendary or apocryphal, but he was my kind of man, and I join thousands of others who are proud to have worked with and for August A. Busch, Jr. His passing in 1989 was a great loss to all who knew him or of him.

CHAPTER 39

A Career Begins

While I had always been aware of Anheuser-Busch and the many advantages attached to working there, my primary concern in life was still the radio broadcasting business. Obviously, in civilian life and in the Army as well, I worked mainly as a radio announcer. However, like most people breaking into the business in those days, I did many other things from time to time. But in my mind they were always temporary jobs while waiting for the "big break." As a result, one of the great surprises of my life was finding myself on the payroll of the Anheuser-Busch Brewery.

I wanted to move into the management and public relations end of the broadcasting business. But I was finding that difficult to do. Most station owners and managers felt that anyone who spent time behind the mike was at best a "Show Biz" type who could never come down to earth long enough to face the problems of a front office. So I let it be known that I was interested in sales, public relations, or whatever it took, in any line, if I could acquire experience which would allow me to get back into broadcasting.

It all came about in the most unusual way. I was in the Anheuser-Busch St. Louis branch office one day, discussing a matter completely unrelated to employment, when the branch supervisor, Mike Shagg, asked me if I had ever thought of going into the beer business. He was talking about a sales position, but he described it as a job dealing with public relations. I learned later that this was not connected with the public relations department, but it did deal with the art of meeting people, making friends, and not necessarily writing orders for beer. I told him I had never thought about it but would like to hear more. After a long discussion, he said he would like me to talk with Jerry Walsh, the St. Louis branch manager, who had the last word on who would be hired. Mr. Walsh was not in at the time, but I was given an application to complete. I filled it out, left it at the office, and went on my way.

I never knew just how they investigated applicants or where they got their background information, but one afternoon several weeks later my wife received a call at our home asking me to be in Jerry Walsh's office the following morning.

Bright and early the next day, I drove the 16 miles from our home in St. Ann, a suburb of St. Louis, to Broadway and Pestalozzi Streets, where the giant brewery City Sales Office was located. It was there that I met with Jerry Walsh.

He was a tall, thin man with grey hair. In my opinion, Jerry could have been mayor of St. Louis if he had so desired. Although I had not met him before, I certainly knew who he was. Everyone knew Jerry Walsh. A veteran of the beer business in St. Louis, Jerry had spent more Anheuser-Busch expense money in taverns, cocktail lounges, restaurants, and at picnics and social affairs than any other person with the company, serving as the brewery's best known emissary. It is inconceivable that anyone who ever visited any of the above didn't at one time or another have a beverage "on Jerry Walsh," even though he had never personally met him. And most of them had actually enjoyed the privilege of shaking his hand and observing his smile as they drank. Jerry always tried to spend at least a few moments with everyone he met. And perhaps one of his most outstanding qualities was that, despite an ailment which caught up with him in later years, causing him pain almost 24 hours a day, no one ever saw him without his famous grin. He was unbelievable.

Jerry seemed to know a lot about me, and in what I later learned was his typical style, he came right to the point. "We have an opening here which I think you can handle very well," he said. "If you're interested, we'd like you to come to work for Anheuser-Busch." After asking a few questions about the job (I knew enough about the company itself), I finally told him I wanted to start. Salary wasn't mentioned but, since I had indicated on the application form what I would accept as a minimum, I felt sure we would have no problems. It was Jerry who brought it up. "I see you've mentioned a starting salary here. Can you and your family get along on that?"

I assured him that the figure was ample. He changed figures on the top and added, "Well, let's make it higher. We don't want you to have to struggle too much." I almost fell off the chair.

I later learned that while he was a generous man, this wasn't just Jerry speaking. This was the overall philosophy of the company. They wanted happy employees. But then I had heard all my life that "Busch takes care of its people." I was thrilled when we agreed I would start in two weeks.

CHAPTER 40

The First Day

On a warm summer morning in 1952, I reported to the personnel department, took my physical, and went through general processing. Then I went back to the City Sales Office and reported for work. Until this time, I was a social drinker only, and was never one to go alone into a tavern "for a few Budweisers," as so many do. Any drink was accompanied by entertainment or dinner, and I was never considered a drinking man. I later discovered that this was one of the things in my favor when I was considered for the job. Obviously, a heavy drinker calling on 12 to 20 bars each day would be looking for trouble.

For openers, I learned that the city branch employed 25 sales people or drummers. The force was separated into two groups: "Off Premise" drummers, who called on grocery and liquor stores where beer could be purchased and taken out, and "On Premise" establishments, where beer was consumed at the point of sale. In St. Louis, this latter meant taverns, cocktail lounges, restaurants, and so on. Jerry soon sent me to train for two weeks with people from both groups. I heard later they were to report back to management on just how I performed and where I would be most valuable.

At this time, one of the "On Premise" people expressed a desire to make a career change. This created a need for either reassignment of an experienced person, and thus perhaps disturbing effectiveness of the staff in two areas, or simply making a single move and putting me in the open spot.

It always amazed me how my predecessor, with such a dream job, could be unhappy in his work. Nevertheless, I felt blessed with a job where you didn't have to search for customers—they were always happy to see the drummer. So I was anxious to hit the street. Mike Shagg told me that Jerry Walsh wanted to see me before I left, so I waited.

Jerry Walsh welcomed me into the office, closed the door, and started to review my first days on the job. He asked such questions as how well I knew certain parts of the city, how my wife felt about my having to put in some night hours on the job, and whether or not I generally liked the work. Apparently I gave the right answers, because Jerry then explained that they were going to make a change in Territory No. 2. I was to be the new drummer!

I spent the rest of the morning with Jerry and Mike. Because I was new, I needed a little training for this job. So I listened to stories of their experience, received pointers on particular owners and managers, and was briefed in general on how to approach the territory.

CHAPTER 41

Territory No. 2

Territory No. 2 covered about 300 on-premise outlets in 20 square miles situated in the approximate center of the St. Louis area: Chouteau to Easton, and Grand west to the city limits. (East St. Louis, just over the Mississippi River in Illinois, was serviced by a distributor who operated his own business.)

Anheuser-Busch generally preferred to work with distributors, but in some areas where the investment expenses and accounts receivable were extremely high, the brewery was forced to operate with its own money. That changed later, when a wholesalership was created in St. Louis proper, and another was authorized for the County. A former

Anheuser-Busch executive, Curt Lohr, was appointed wholesaler in St. Louis proper, and another, Tom Burrows, was chosen to operate in St. Louis County.

Mike Shagg took me to coffee, where we could talk before starting on the street. He then took me to the key spots in the territory where large volumes of our Budweiser and Michelob products were sold. He also introduced me to some of the people I would be dealing with for the next few years. It is interesting to note some of the instructions he gave me. These, and certain other factors pointed out later, are what made the beer drummer's job so unusual.

Mike's advice was thorough.

"Remember that you *are* Anheuser-Busch in this territory. Every item of our brewery division sold here will be credited to you. However, there are no quotas. Budweiser products sell themselves. You need only sell Dick Wall. You never carry any of the product with you. The trucks on the street make all deliveries. Be friendly with the truck drivers. They can help you tremendously. They stop two or three times a week, while you'll be there less frequently. If a retailer is unhappy, or when the competitive drummer is making headway with him, your driver will let you know. Never let the driver buy a lunch or drink, and never forget to give him a birthday and Christmas present. He's your friend." I had a lot of friends, because it took approximately 15 trucks to service the route.

Mike taught me more about the business in a few weeks than an ordinary teacher could have imparted in a lifetime. With a limited education, he had risen from truck driver to drummer and then to supervisor. There was little he didn't know about the beer business. A sharp dresser, but wearing clothes designed to get the most out of a size 46-inch waist, Mike could go with the best. He spoke with a slight German accent, as did many South St. Louis people. With a big cigar in his mouth most of the time, he was never without a comeback.

He gave me a copy of a book called *Making Friends Is Our Business,* which related the story of the Anheuser and Busch families and how they formed and developed this great corporation. Mike told me the title also described the philosophy of the entire organization. He repeated his earlier words: Sell yourself and make friends.

CHAPTER 42

Life at the Branch

While I have conceded that drummers were an unusual lot, even more unusual were the varied backgrounds of those selected for the jobs.

From baseball, music, law enforcement, food merchandising, advertising and, of course, radio, plus almost any other field you can imagine, came this unique group in St. Louis City Sales.

Red Kasper, Don Brogan, Jim Kroll, Vince Brencik, Mel Mueller, Jimmy Dunn, Al Lucas, Ray Heaven, Bernie Schulte, Bob Hayward, Bob Martin and Jim Jeter made up a partial list of Jerry Walsh's talented crew.

Jim Jeter was a great example of how a person could make the transition from another line of work to beer drumming.

Jim had for years been well known to many St. Louisans. He directed the popular Jeter Pillars Orchestra at the famous Plantation Nightclub. When Anheuser-Busch offered Jim a chance to join City Sales, he made the change from show business and was a great success. His retailers loved him, and there wasn't a more popular man in our office.

Territory No. 2 was unlike most. I had 300 outlets to call on and service, but they were situated in diversified areas. They included some of the leading hotels in St. Louis, fashionable restaurants and cocktail lounges on the Old Debaliviere Strip, small bars and grills in the industrial areas, the regular neighborhood taverns, and even the lower class saloons. Some of those were frequented by ladies of the evening and their "managers," as well as by petty thieves and burglars. And, of course, I had my share of outlets frequented by sports celebrities, media people and police officers. People from "all walks of life" was never a more appropriate expression. Almost without exception, I was accepted by the principals as friend and confidant because I was a drummer. As a result, no day was ordinary. My job was to visit 12-15 such places each day so that, on a five-day-per-week basis, I would see the owners or operators and some of their patrons at least once a month.

The schedule of each of the 25 drummers varied somewhat, but generally our duties were the same. Two days each week (Monday and Thursday in my case) I reported to the office in our St. Louis branch at Broadway and

Pestalozzi. I turned in my report and expense sheet, picked up expense money to carry me through the next period on the street, and obtained a supply of calendars, napkins, coasters or other point-of-purchase material for distribution to the operators I would visit during the next two or three days.

I was equipped with a few rules and regulations and had guidelines within which to work. But I handled Territory No. 2 pretty much as I saw fit. I was given an advance of "bar spending money," with instructions that it was against the law to spend any of it for improvement of retail outlets, painting signs, bribery, etc. The money could only be used for sampling the product. This meant that I could ask people in an outlet to "try a bottle of Bud," or I could have a drink myself in an effort to see that the product was fresh and properly served. While in an outlet, we were urged to check in the storeroom or cooler and to rotate the product if necessary (to assure each consumer that the Bud was as fresh as it could be). Incidentally, few people realized that on each container and on each case of Bud beer there was a code which gave the date the beer was packaged. From this code the drummer could tell how fresh the product was. Contrary to popular belief, beer doesn't age or improve in the bottle or can.

This great concern for the quality of our product extended not only to the specially trained drummers, but to other employees as well, especially when they became consumers in their own neighborhoods. Many men and women employed in the "House of Anheuser-Busch" exhibited keen interest in product quality maintenance. They demonstrated this interest by checking the codes on cans and bottles in their neighborhood bars, restaurants and stores. They weren't paid for this interest. They simply cared.

CHAPTER 43

Trained to Sell

No other brewery offered a training program for sales and public relations people like Anheuser-Busch! Just sending a person out to glad-hand and buy drinks fell far short of the high standards held by this great organization. Annual tours of the brewery and a steady supply of product information, coupled with the drummers' detailed knowledge of company and industry history, placed Anheuser-Busch drummers in a most advantageous position within the marketplace. Management knew that people not only ask questions about ingredients and the aging of beer and other products, but they also inquire about the families who put it all together. Our people were equipped to answer most of those questions.

The company's history began with establishment of the Bavarian Brewery by George Schneider, who owned the business from 1852 through 1860. Eberhard Anheuser then assumed ownership of St. Louis' 29th ranked brewery (in a market of 40) and renamed it Eberhard Anheuser and Company Bavarian Brewery. He introduced Budweiser in 1876. (Adolphus Busch married Lilly Anheuser in 1861, thereby uniting these two great families.) Every dedicated Anheuser-Busch person knew the story. Each person would also point out that, although Bud was brewed by Eberhard Anheuser and Company, it was bottled and distributed by Carl Conrad at that time.

Michelob came along (but only on tap) in 1896. Many St. Louisans were interested in facts about the company and the families who made the big machine go. In my estimation the most frequently asked questions would include:

(1) What's the story of the "A and Eagle" trademark?

It became the trademark in 1877, and to this day reflects that the A is for Anheuser, and an American Eagle soars at the highest levels, knowing no limitations. That describes Anheuser-Busch.

(2) Where does the name "Budweiser" come from?

The word Budweiser, as applied to Anheuser-Busch beer, was thought by some to have derived from an association with a medieval city in Europe. It was actually Adolphus Busch, however, who chose the name "Budweiser" for his new lager beer. He did so because it sounded European but was easily pronounced by Americans. Michelob was named in a similar fashion, and Bud and Mick became household terms quite easily.

(3) Was Michelob always sold in bottles?

As noted earlier, Michelob was introduced as a draft beer in 1896, and in 1961 it was sold in bottles for the first time.

On any given day, a drummer would be asked the above questions at least once—and the questions took off from there. And believe me, the public is still fascinated by this fabulous story.

CHAPTER 44

Product Knowledge

Shortly after my assignment, I was sent to a brewery-operated school taught by knowledgeable, dedicated people. It was their responsibility to train persons in how beer was made, how it should be served, and how to merchandise it in the retail outlet. As a result, Anheuser-Busch drummers received excellent instruction and were probably the best prepared sales people in the industry. This approach didn't stop at the brewery. Distributors, or "wholesalers" as Anheuser-Busch liked to call them, were also exposed to this information, and many traveled hundreds of miles from their markets to take this full-week course at the brewery.

Instructors included chemists and brewmasters on the product side, while experienced sales and merchandising people taught the art of getting distribution in the outlet. They even trained people in the building of those beer displays you have seen in your supermarket or beverage store. Everything began with a tour of the world's largest brewery. Anheuser-Busch maintains a large staff of professional guides who routinely escort consumers through the brewery. But our guide was a man who attended brewmaster school and who really gave us a concise picture of what is done and why it is done. The tour took the greater part of the first day.

Dick Wall (seated in center) with colleagues at the Anheuser-Busch, Inc., Sales School on December 17, 1953.

Most people never saw the inside of the draft beer school on the second floor of the old Bevo plant at Broadway and Pestalozzi. ("Bevo" was the nonalcoholic beverage sold by Anheuser-Busch during Prohibition.) This was just across the street from the City Sales Office, where I would later headquarter. Under the guidance of B. H. Nissen and Walter Telle, the school operated like a regular high school or college. A staff of instructors led classes from 15 to 25 students. Each course was scheduled for a specific time and lasted until the group moved into another area of instruction. From inside, one would think he or she were in a grocery store or bar: not only was beer in the coolers and on the shelves, but other food products and signs were on display to lend authenticity to the scene.

Since no establishment should carry "unfresh beer," the drummer was under standing orders to confiscate the product as soon as he saw something that didn't toe the mark. If there were just a few cans or bottles, or even a case, he would buy it at retail and take it from the premises, taking care to pour it out so that no one was able to drink it. The beer would not make one ill, but it certainly wouldn't taste its best, and it obviously wouldn't prompt the drinker to order the same brand next time. Shelf life of our beer was about 60 days. After that time, it was not harmful but it also was no longer at its best.

Along with several police officers and other citizens, I will never forget a hot day in August many years ago. During a routine call on a retail outlet, I discovered a few six-packs of Bud which, according to their package dates, were considered unfresh. This was beer that was drinkable but not at its best. A porter who was responsible for rotating beverages had apparently slipped up and created a small problem.

The Anheuser-Busch training program kicked in, and the situation was corrected. I purchased the six-packs to get them off the market. So I paid full price to the retailer, placed it in the trunk of my car, and drove to Forest Park, stopping near a sewer. Sitting on the curb, I started the slow process of pouring cans of Bud into the gutter. Dozens of cars passed, each slowing to take a closer look at what I was doing. As the hot brew began to foam over the curb, many people offered to take the Bud off my hands. I soon stopped trying to explain, until a squad of bluecoats pulled up and asked me the same old question.

I responded with the same old answer, "I'm pouring this beer in the sewer." Saying they had several complaints about some nut in the park just pouring beer in the street, one cop even wanted to handcuff me and take me in. I went through the whole story of aged beer and finally convinced them that everyone would be better off if they would enjoy a few cold ones later as my guest. They drove off happy but shaking their heads.

CHAPTER 45

Do You Remember
These Old Breweries?

- American — General Offices, 2835 South Broadway

- Anheuser-Busch — 9th and Pestalozzi

- Anheuser-Busch — Western Depot, 3533 Evans Ave.

- Brinkwirth-Nolker — 18th and Cass

- City — 14th and Chambers

- Columbia — 20th and Madison

- Consumers' — Shenandoah and Lemp

- Empire — Sarah and Wabash Tracks

- Excelsior — 5 South 17th

- Forest Park — 3662 Forest Park Blvd.

- Gast — Office and Depot, Broadway and Cass

- Gast — 8501 N. Broadway

- Green Tree — 9th and Sidney

- Griesedieck — 1920 Shenandoah

- Grone — 2219 Clark

- Home — 3600 Salena St.

- Hyde Park — Salisbury and Florissant

- Klausmann — 8539 S. Broadway

- Lafayette — 18th and Cass

- Lemp — 13th and Cherokee

- Milwaukee-Woukesha — 2939 January

- Mutual — Boyle and Duncan Ave.

- National — 18th and Gratiot

- Obert — 12th and McGirk

- Phoenix — 1725 Lafayette

- Schlitz — Carr and Collins

- Shorr-Kolkschneider — Parnell and Natural Bridge

CHAPTER 46

The Debaliviere Strip

The Debaliviere Strip was as lively a row of fine restaurants and cocktail lounges as you could have found in
the '50s. Running from Delmar to the edge of Forest Park
at the Jefferson Memorial, it was a beer drummer's dream.
Only a few of the 15 drinking and eating establishments
opened before 11 a.m. They were called on and serviced
properly, but there were few consumers in them at that time
of day. So it was just a matter of having a drink with customers and going on my way. But I always managed to call
back at night.

I had my choice of places for lunch too. Stan Musial,
the old Cardinals star, owned an excellent businessman's

lunch spot. Kayo Koverly, the former boxing and wrestling great, operated a plush restaurant that served excellent lunches and dinners. It was always fun to call on Kayo. He didn't sell a great deal of beer, handling largely cocktails and highballs, but the largest share of beer sold at his place was Bud.

Tommy George's at Debaliviere and Waterman was a late nightspot where the best dressed men and women always congregated. From secretary to socialite, salesman, business executive, doctor or lawyer, you'd find them at Tommy's Sorrentos. His good food and drink, along with the irrepressible personality of Tommy himself, literally packed them in.

The Tic Tock Tap was another late spot. A place for an out-of-the-way table or booth during the day, it changed to a top flight nightclub after six. And the Mural Room just across from Sorrentos was another.

There were many more, and the Strip always offered excitement. Without identifying some of the others, it's fair to say they helped create such a cross section of entertainment that anyone could have a good time there, from early morning until closing in the wee hours of the following day. One could sip a drink, knowing that pleasant conversation, sports talk, horse betting, pretty girls, anything he wanted was only a few minutes away in one direction or another. No trash, no troublemakers, no brawls—it was St. Louis at its entertaining best. From love songs to Dixieland, if you wanted it, you got it.

Then an undesirable element crept in. Slowly the discreet girls on appointment were replaced by hardened "street hustlers." Top level entertainment gave way to vulgar dancers and comics. And soon the clientele changed from ladies and gentlemen to a less refined group, which made it inadvisable to take your wife or best girl into the area at night.

A drive down the old Strip just a few years ago would have broken the heart of a patron. Massage parlors, boarded-up stores, broken windows and dirty sidewalks made it difficult to imagine what once was there. What formerly took two days of exciting brewery calls probably took the drummer of recent years less than an hour to cover. Some people tried to restore it, but "the Strip was gone" and will never again be the same.

Oldtimers, however, watch with great interest as concerned citizens try to bring the old neighborhood back.

CHAPTER 47

Gaslight Square

I received a call one day from a man who had not been in the bar business. But he had an idea and wanted to talk about it. His name was Richard Mutrux. He was opening a new cocktail lounge at Boyle and Olive. I quickly went to see him.

There were two or three taverns in the neighborhood, serving a less-than-upscale clientele. I had called on them for some time, since this was part of my territory. And I knew the owners to be dependable, honest guys. Their only problem was they were in a neighborhood that for a long time had been the heart of the red light district. Their trade was "blue shirt or no shirts" from the area, plus a few Westside dudes who occasionally stopped in for a drink and a hooker.

For Richard Mutrux, this was a problem, because he was looking for the type of customer who had made up the original Debaliviere Strip. Richard didn't need advice from me on people. He simply wanted to know what brands of beer to stock. He knew he would be catering to the "Cocktail Set," but felt he should have beer as well. I looked at his cooler space and advised him to handle only two beers, Budweiser and another I have forgotten by now.

Richard, with the cooperation of several local businessmen—Jay Landesman, Marty Bronson and others—slowly organized what was to be known nationally as "Gaslight Square," the name derived from Mutrux's "Gaslight." Nothing like Gaslight Square had ever been imagined in St. Louis, or anywhere else in the country for that matter. Gourmet restaurants, nightclubs, bars and antique shops literally put St. Louis on the map again. Running from Whittier Street to Walton, Olive Street was the entertainment center of the Midwest. The area covered only a few blocks east and west, but it soon spread several blocks to the south on Boyle. Eventually, entrepreneurs were exploiting other streets running parallel to Olive.

I left St. Louis before the real heyday of Gaslight Square. But I visited the development many times, only to stand amazed. Here were literally thousands of people filling the outlets and spilling onto the streets, so that streetcars and automobile traffic had to be rerouted. Every night was like Mardi Gras. St. Louisans loved it, and the operators practically coined money.

Local people soon were augmented by tourists, and the streets became even more crowded. Gaslight Square was high on every visitor's "Things to See" list. Anyone who ever visited Gaslight Square will never forget it. I recall starting an evening with cocktails at Mutrux's Gaslight, having dinner in one of several fine restaurants offering a choice of American, Greek, Japanese, Italian and other foreign delicacies, and then moving on to Marty's, a drinking establishment operated by St. Louis television and night-club star Marty Bronson.

Marty offered old world atmosphere and delicious beverages, served by some of the most talented men and women you could find. They were either professional singers before coming there, or they were studying voice and theatre. On a given evening, the patrons could refresh and hear songs ranging from light opera to the heavy stuff, always highlighted by Marty's own repertoire. His most frequently requested number was "If Ever I Would Leave You."

A late night show was only a few hundred feet away. This was at Davey's, where part of the same crowd jammed the club to see and hear Davey Bold, a pianist, singer and comedian. Davey was one of the funniest men in the country. And while he had worked Vegas and gone over well, he preferred the Midwest. And I might add, the Midwest loved him.

Davey loved to tell this story about the actual sharpness of the Rural Lad, often described by some big city fellows as "dumb."

A young lady from the big city was invited to spend part of her summer vacation on a farm owned by the father of one of her girlfriends. After several days, she decided to take a walk around the area and just relax, all by herself, and soak up some of the rural atmosphere.

While strolling down a road, she came across a lazy stream, where she stopped, just to sit down on the bank and unwind. The thought of a refreshing swim in the cool water occurred to her, but since she hadn't brought a swimsuit with her, she quickly ruled out entering the water. Soon it dawned on her that she was alone, and there was no one nearby to see her, so she decided to have a dip in her birthday suit. She took off her clothes, folded them neatly, placed them on the bank, and slowly entered the water. After a brief stay in the stream, and now feeling completely relaxed, she approached her clothing and began to wade out toward the bank.

To her amazement, a young farm boy was seated next to the spot where she had left her garments. Without saying a word, he just stared at her! As she approached the edge of the water, she was grateful to stumble on a rusty old dishpan lying in the gravel at the bottom of the water. Feeling a bit more confident, she reached down, picked up the dishpan, held it up in front of her and boldly waded out of the stream and walked toward the young man, who said nothing but continued to look at her.

Her confidence slowly changed to anger, and in a fury she said, *"Look, you, do you know what I think?"*

The lad, with all the courtesy he could muster, replied, "Yes, ma'am, I know what you think. You think there's a bottom in that old dishpan!"

CHAPTER 48

The End of Gaslight Square

Jay Landesman operated a smart club on Olive Street where the crowds were able to enjoy many struggling performers who went on to national fame. Shelly Berman and the Smothers Brothers are some who come to mind. Yes, Gaslight Square was great, and it became greater over a period of several years.

Then something happened. An undesirable element drifted into the area. Some called it the "beginning of the end," referring to the discovery that pickpockets and purse snatchers began to mingle in the huge crowds. Vandals, car thieves and holdup men took over the parking lots, and soon the townsfolk began to find safer places to go. Men refused to take their wives or dates into the area. Obviously, it didn't take long for visitors to get the word. As business fell off, so did profits, and the area faded away. Drive through there in recent years (you wouldn't want to walk), and you won't believe the shambles and devastation that once was Gaslight Square. Civic leaders predict redevelopment of the neighborhood, but we shall see.

CHAPTER 49

Busch Lager

Forest Park Boulevard was a part of my territory, although there were no restaurants or bars on that street between Kingshighway and Grand. One unusual account I called on was in the offices of the Falstaff Brewery. The brewery was actually located in South St. Louis, but they had offices, storage space and other phases of the brewery in this part of my territory. I used to stop in there once a month because they were nice people who always got a laugh when I'd ask, "How many cases of Budweiser do you need today?" Falstaff, of course, maintained a license at this location so that, from time to time, they could service special customers with some of their product.

Also in that area were several printing companies, one of which dealt in package labels. Another nearby company manufactured bottle caps, or "crowns" as they were known in the trade. Several times I was asked if we were coming out with a new beer. I simply told them that we weren't about to bring a new beer on the market, and let it go at that. Soon rumors to the contrary were brought into our sales meeting from people who worked miles from where the questions had been asked of me. Management had simply said there was no credence to the rumors. Still, my colleagues and I felt more and more that we were going to introduce a new popular-priced beer. But our Busch people denied it. Jerry Walsh, the branch manager, said to forget it. "If we were going to bring out a new beer, I'd know it." Soon John Hallquist, one of the top executives of the brewery, came to our office. At a special meeting, he assured all employees in the branch that there were no plans such as we had heard on the street.

Not long after that meeting, I was in one of our draft outlets at Newstead and Laclede, where I got the surprise of my life. After I once again answered questions on the subject, a fellow offered to bet me that I was wrong. You could have knocked me over with a Budweiser napkin when this customer presented me with a label and a crown which he brought in from his place of work. There it was: *Busch Lager Beer*, bottled by Anheuser-Busch in St. Louis— and after months of denial by top people in the organization. I hurried to the office, showed the label and crown, and Mr. Hallquist simply said, "There is nothing to it."

Well, the cat was out of the bag, and no one would discuss it. It was several weeks later, with still no confirmation, when I received word that there would be a meeting of all branch personnel that day at 5 p.m. We all reported in, really not knowing what to expect, since inquiries had been put to rest relative to a new beer. When we walked into the office, there they were—signs, coasters, napkins—all promoting Busch Lager Beer, despite all that went before. We were shocked.

Executives showed us newspaper ads due to come out the following morning introducing Busch Lager—a popular-priced beer and companion to our great premium brew, Budweiser. (Michelob was only on draft in those days.) The Busch Lager was being loaded onto trucks for delivery the next day. We were to hit the streets and promote it, asking people to sample the beer, which was as different from Bud as they could make it. It would sell for a nickel less than our premium product, Budweiser. The next step was to ask all of us to sample Busch Lager—something we couldn't wait to do. Naturally, we found it different. So it was hard to get an honest opinion, though enthusiasm bubbled everywhere in the office. Each of us was given a case of Busch Lager to take home and try with our family. I took mine to my mom and dad's, where we all became enthused, as I knew we would.

About three hours later I had a call from my dad. He was all for Anheuser-Busch, as you know from my earlier comments in this book. But he apologetically said, "It won't hold a collar." In layman's language, this means it won't retain foam after being poured into a glass. Ads ran in the St. Louis papers the next day. The product was there, and we started promoting it. Another meeting was called that evening so that management could get a report on the reaction of customers in St. Louis. (The beer was introduced only in the St. Louis metro area.) Most of us were excited and said so. Someone finally mentioned, however, that he and other people that day had noticed that the beer wouldn't hold a collar. Shortly, other drummers began to admit they had run into that same problem. They were sure, however, that this occurred only because of the newness of Busch Lager. Maybe it wasn't aged as long as Bud and so on. Sales took off when we tried to promote the beer, but the old collar complaint continued. Advertising went on but, as we all knew, there was a problem somewhere. John Hallquist would call meetings to tell us how to pour the beer. He insisted that, where we had a complaint, perhaps the glasses were not "beer clean." We listened, but we also cited examples of Budweiser doing just what it should do, and in glasses washed the same way. As sales began to fall, we soon discontinued production. Busch Lager died a quiet death—almost as quiet as its birth. This is the only major mistake I've ever known Anheuser-Busch to make. I've often wondered if the attempt to blitz the market in utter secrecy, to deny the coming of the beer, was purely the strategy of one person. Or were all of our top agency and brewery people in on it? I don't know. Busch Lager, born in March of 1955, was withdrawn in November of 1955. *Requiescat in pace!*

Jim Barsi, our talented national sales manager, left the brewery shortly after this incident. Somehow, I knew that Mr. Busch would come up with a winner in a hurry. Because when he enters the arena, he enters to win, and I knew it wouldn't take long.

CHAPTER 50

Bud Draft Beer—Why Not?

Every drummer is familiar with the procedure for qualifying a prospect. Anyone considered a prospect must have both the authority to buy and sufficient money or credit with which to buy. There are many ways to apply this formula effectively, plus a few ways to misapply it.

As a rule, our sales and merchandising school (where I spent some time on the faculty) offered no scheduled or organized classes during June, July and August, because most wholesalers were busy in their own markets. We instructors often received assignments to travel into markets where we might be of service to wholesalers, while at the same time observing our classroom suggestions in action.

Sometimes what works in a given market will also do very well in other markets, and then—sometimes not.

It was our practice, when entering the market, to talk with a wholesaler in order to discover any special problems which we might help him solve. After an initial meeting, we would join the wholesaler or one of his people and make calls on retailers. My preference was to visit outlets which, for one reason or another, did not handle our product, though I always went there with the local people. Experience taught me that our hosts usually wanted to visit outlets where they were well known, and where Anheuser-Busch point-of-purchase materials were plentiful. But that didn't bother me. Eventually we would come upon spots where I could be of service.

Talking with hundreds of retailers over the years, I felt I had heard every excuse in the world for not serving Bud on Draft. But I was wrong, as the following story shows.

It has been said that "the best beer salesman in the world is a hot day in August." It was during one of those hot weeks that I was helping the wholesaler in a small Texas town.

In this tiny community, we found a bar which might profit from serving Bud on Draft, and I felt I could supply several reasons why it should.

After inviting consumers present to sample our Bud in bottles, I shook hands with each customer. I then turned to the owner and began to itemize the advantages of Bud on Draft. I explained that he would get more glasses of Bud out of our half-barrels with the "Golden Gate" tap. For openers, this meant greater profit. In addition, the Golden

Gate tap was actually safer than the Peerless tap. The bar owner, however, wasn't impressed.

I then pointed to the fresh quality of our Bud, which meant a better taste. This in turn would prompt consumers to enjoy an extra glass without getting that filled-up feeling. No sale!

Didn't the owner see the prospect of new customers brought in by the large Bud sign outside? He wasn't sure about that!

After pointing to several other facts that have led to more successful operations all over the country, I began to feel that I was losing this battle. I reviewed the points already mentioned and then landed my knockout punch:

"More customers, fresher beer, safer taps, the outside sign and, finally, more profit! Doesn't that seem important to you?"

"No," he said.

"My question, sir, is why not?" I asked.

Without hesitation, the owner came back with a response I had never considered but would never forget.

"All of the points you've made may be true," the bar owner said. "But my reason for not taking on Bud Draft is a simple one. My present draft beer wholesaler owns this building, and my lease is up for renewal next month!"

Enough said.

CHAPTER 51

Joe Corelli

One of the advantages of living more than 75 years, as I have, is that you learn a few things along the way. One of the most valuable lessons I learned while drumming for Anheuser-Busch was to make up my own mind about people, and not just blindly believe what newspapers and members of the general public said about them. If no man is an island, then no man is totally evil either. Human nature being what it is, all of us have varying mixtures of good and bad elements in our character. And so it was with Joe Corelli.

From an early age, Joe encountered a less-than-whole-some side of life. One of his aunts, for example, ran an establishment that received regular visits from the vice squad. And as Joe grew older, he had his own brushes with the law. Although I never met Joe until I became a drummer, I had heard and read about him for many years. Joe had a reputation, and it wasn't good. But in the performance of my duties, I came to know Joe as a consumer, and I had shaken his hand many times. I found him to be an ordinary fellow who seemed to mind his own business and to function as a listener rather than a talker.

I remember calling for several weeks on Carl, a particular retailer. My goal was to persuade him to carry Bud Draft Beer, but I had been unsuccessful. After five or six visits, however, on stops made during the quiet of an afternoon when business was slow, I noticed that Joe was always seated in a booth when I arrived. He remained quiet but, when I made my presentations, it was obvious that he was listening. Joe was a spectator, but an interested one. I wondered why. He was always present during my calls, yet wasn't a heavy drinker or big talker. When Joe did speak, it was softly. He sounded like anything but a hardened criminal. Joe had a felony conviction, however, so I knew he was prohibited by law from serving as an owner of the bar.

One summer day, I made another visit to Carl, whose name was listed as the establishment's owner. Carl became annoyed at my sales pitch and, in a strong voice, gave me what he described as his final "No." As I prepared to leave, Joe said to Carl in a soft but authoritative tone: "This young guy has worked hard doing his job, and what he says makes a lot of sense. I think you ought to give him a chance and put in Bud Draft."

Was Joe a behind-the-scenes owner? Was he a silent partner? Joe is gone now, so we'll never really know. But I do remember Carl's reaction to Joe's advice.

"O.K., Joe," was his smiling but deferential reply. Turning to me, Carl sprang the surprise of my life when he said:

"Dick, how soon can we start to serve Bud on Draft?"

Despite the bad reputation that preceded him, Joe Corelli showed that he too had a softer side. In retrospect, I'm glad I had a chance to see that facet of his personality. I wonder how many others who knew Joe Corelli reserved judgment and recall him today as the warm, soft-spoken man he could sometimes be—a guy who had the capacity to care about people.

CHAPTER 52

Draft Stop

In those days of the 1950s, most breweries were trying to increase their number of "draft stops," which are on-premise outlets serving draft beer.

The thought behind all of the effort to get Budweiser or Michelob served in as many places as practical was a simple one.

The "on tap" sign meant not only draft beer sales, but a larger share of the packaged beer served in the outlet. The outside sign brought people in, and the cash register sign plus other point-of-sale material helped greatly. Bud and Mick, as Budweiser and Michelob are sometimes called, were served in most of the finer bars and restaurants in St.

Louis. And every drummer had a list of people in his territory who wanted to serve the finest draft beer in the world. But it would hardly be good business to saturate every corner with draft stops. So we had all of the key outlets. And except for unusual cases, this was all we cared to handle.

Despite the above, I once had a bar operator who wanted to improve his business and his clientele, so he asked me about our draft beer. Because Michelob stops were usually premium outlets, I talked to him for several weeks regarding Bud on Draft. I was new in the business, and if we took him on, he would be the first draft stop I had collared.

But before I gave my okay, I checked with St. Louis' number one draft authority, Mike Shagg, who was the assistant sales manager in our St. Louis branch. He offered to make a call on the bar with me. I gave him all the information I had, and I hoped he would agree that we should go ahead. As we entered, I approached the owner, who was seated at the bar. To my surprise, Mike walked toward the restroom area.

In a few minutes, he joined us to talk. It seemed he wasn't as enthused as I was. With reference to several minor problems, Mike was most polite in pointing them out to the operator. He urged that his suggestions about the lighting in the bar, the air conditioning and general decor be observed. Mike surprised both the owner and me, however, when he mentioned the restrooms. Mike insisted that the restrooms be kept clean at all times. We agreed that we'd all get together in 30 days or so and talk again.

As Mike and I drove away, I realized how right he was. "Always remember," he said to me, "if the place isn't clean, particularly the restrooms, then they can't serve our draft beer as it should be served. Remember what we've always taught you—Bud is a food product, and we keep it fresh. It should never be contaminated by anything. Check the restroom every time, and if the restroom ain't clean, the whole outlet ain't clean."

The 30 days came, and our talks continued. But the draft beer picture in that bar never changed because some people, at least people like that bar owner, never change.

CHAPTER 53

Tommy Bugg

One of the best saloon operators I ever knew was Tommy Bugg. He operated a clean place at the corner of Boyle and Maryland, just south of Gaslight Square. It wasn't unusual to meet high-ranking police officers, bookmakers, gamblers, ladies of the evening, entertainers, newspaper reporters and athletes all at one time in Tommy's place. He knew them all. And with his gift of gab, Tommy never made an enemy. This was one of the places where secrets stayed between the walls. What might be called "gossip" in some bars was never repeated outside Tommy Bugg's.

It was not commonplace, but from time to time the beer drummer received a ticket for overparking. This occurred because, when he parked his car, he never knew just how long he would be away from it. It occurred infrequently to me, because most cops recognized my car and would usually give me a break. As a result, if I found a ticket on my windshield, I never got excited. In a day or two, the officer who inadvertently wrote it would most likely pick it up and take the citation off my hands. If I did accumulate a ticket or two, I would give it to Tommy, and he would know how to handle it.

One day I received a letter from the police department. There apparently were several tickets issued to my license plate, and none had been taken care of. The letter said that I should report to the department within five days to clear up the situation. I casually mentioned this to Tommy, who quickly said, "Give me the letter and I'll give it to —." Then he named one of the top St. Louis politicians who would take care of the case. "Forget about it," Tom said. And I did.

One fine day, I was driving east on Olive, approaching Vandeventer, when I saw flashing lights and heard the growl of the siren from a police cruiser. I pulled across the intersection and stopped, only to learn that the officers were Phoebe and Carol. They were two of the first women to go into full-time police work. This meant they were not meter maids, but big league pistol-packing cops. And they were after me!

Phoebe was all business. She told me I was on the "hot sheet" and therefore under arrest. Carol appeared satisfied to let me off with a warning. Phoebe, however, insisted that they take me in.

In crossing Vandeventer, I had driven from the 11th Police District into the 6th District. This meant I had to go to a station with which I wasn't too familiar. I knew that in the 11th, at Newstead and Laclede, I would have been among friends. But it turned out that the desk clerk and lieutenant on duty in the 6th knew me. On a few occasions, they had even "sampled my product" at a nearby watering hole.

I assumed I would wait in the outer office of the 6th District. Phoebe, however, insisted that I go into the "holdover" until making bond. As it was, the lieutenant questioned me in his comfortable office until bond could be posted. This allowed me to avoid waiting in the tank where Phoebe had wanted to send me.

After talking with the lieutenant for a few minutes, it was decided I would not be detained at all, and that bond would not be necessary. As I left the station, I headed straight for Tommy's Bar to see what my next move should be. When I told Tommy what had happened, he insisted that I let him continue to handle the matter. Phoebe, in her enthusiasm to follow through, had in the meantime charged me with 17 separate parking violations. This began to look serious. I was worried, but I again trusted Tom to talk with one of his high-level politicians, who would wrap it up.

I didn't hear from Tommy for about ten days, so I went in to see him. I asked where we stood and how our ticket thing was going. Tommy said, "We'll have to go a different route to get this thing straightened out."

"Why, Tom, what's the delay?" I asked him.

Without any apology or stalling, he told me very plainly, "We have to make other plans because my top guy, who was going to fix this for you, my ace politician, is in jail!"

I later secured a lawyer. With his help, I pleaded guilty, paid a $22 fine, and walked away a free man.

George Huebner

George Huebner is one of the most interesting people I know. Forty years ago, he was a handsome, young Kansas City bachelor who worked as a drummer there. I had met him at brewery meetings and conventions but didn't know him very well.

We became better acquainted when we were both assigned to travel throughout the South, introducing Busch Bavarian Beer. As reported elsewhere, our general approach was to meet with wholesalers and their people. We would make retail calls with some of them, and then point out sales strategies that might help as they introduced the new Anheuser-Busch product. George was an excellent drummer. Heavy set, with a loud voice, he could enter an outlet and within a few minutes have most of the customers learning all about Busch Bavarian Beer.

In one small town in Missouri, we made a call on a drugstore that carried many brands of beer. Largely through George's salesmanship, it took on our product too. After completing our business, George asked the druggist if he would wrap some chocolates for him. He wanted a two-pound box, a five-pound box and a ten-pound box of chocolates, each wrapped separately. The druggist handed George his packages and, smiling, said, "You must really like chocolates!"

George returned the smile, adding, "No, I'm not really crazy about candy, but I'll let you in on a secret. When I visit a small town like this, I usually take candy with me, go out to the local shopping area and find a young lady who is willing to join me for dinner and a movie. At the movie we sometimes do a little kissing, you know, and if she is cuddly, I give her a two-pound box of candy—and if she is a little more affectionate, I give her the five-pound box, and then if she's really cool, I give her the whole thing— two pounds, five pounds and ten pounds of candy."

The druggist thanked us and we left.

George went out to the shopping district and, as usual, met a sweet young thing who agreed to go with him to dinner and a movie. She went home to change, and George picked her up an hour later.

She invited him to meet the members of her family, who were just beginning their dinner. The girl's dad asked George to say grace.

George complied. He asked God's blessing on the food, the family, the farmer who grew the food, and the grocer who delivered it. He prayed for everyone. George was superb!

When George and the girl walked toward his car, she seemed delighted. She held his arm and said, "I'm so proud of the way you prayed with my family. But I didn't know you were so religious."

George's only comment was, "I didn't know your dad was the druggist."

Bob Shunick

Bob Shunick is a very talented person. He came out of the small town of Monmouth, Illinois, and joined Anheuser-Busch in St. Louis as a drummer. Because he was so flexible, he was used mainly as a utility person. On premise or off premise, he could step in and replace any one of us for a day or two or a week. He just met people so well that he was liked by fellow drummers, management, wholesalers and retailers.

But I suppose his longest suit was his strong sense of humor and his ability to do impressions. And not the least of these was his impression of Mr. August A. Busch, Jr.

Most of us in the St. Louis branch had heard Bob "do" Mr. Busch, but his reputation was soon recognized "up the street" at the executive offices as well.

Bob and I had written a script based on the old Dragnet television format. It turned out to be a very funny piece, using the "da da dum dum" opening and featuring Bob and me as beer drummers instead of Joe Friday and his detective partner.

The title was "Draft Beer, the Documented Story of Your Beer Drummer in Action, etc., etc." With the familiar theme in the background, Bob and I traveled step by step as beer drummers for ten minutes or more. We answered complaints about everything from warm beer and dirty glasses to unfresh beer. Finally, in our story at least, we were directed to call upon Mr. Busch. As I spoke for both of us, Bob took over as Mr. Busch. "Mr. Busch" discussed the

*Bob Shunick
with
Dick Wall.*

brewery and its history, his "Good Daddy," the New Orleans story, and our competitors—all "take-offs" on talks the real Mr. Busch had actually made, and all familiar to Anheuser-Busch sales employees.

All of our people, including wholesalers, would recognize the message and voice. It was so similar to Mr. Busch's that it made the tape a winner.

We introduced it at a branch Christmas party to give our own people a laugh. What we didn't expect was that Walter Telle, a longtime employee and friend of Mr. Busch, took our only copy of the tape to the executive Christmas party. Everyone there roared at the humor and accuracy. But the biggest laughs came from Mr. Busch himself. He liked it so well, I'm told, that he kept the tape for his personal collection.

Mr. Busch sent for Shunick and me. The two of us received compliments from the big boss. From what I hear, he played that tape for close friends over the course of many, many years.

CHAPTER 56

Legend

I don't know what a poll would reveal, but I'm certain a fair amount of people in this country would admit to a perception that some bartenders are less than 100% honest when it comes to handling cash coming across the bar.

I personally never observed any misconduct, but then I was never in a bar for that purpose. For that matter, one of the going jokes a few years ago related to persons in *all* retail outlets where a cash register was involved:

"Hey, do you know the 'Cash Register Song'?"
"No, what is the 'Cash Register Song'?"
"It's called 'This Place Will Soon Be Mine.'"

But a story making the rounds when I was in and out of saloons went something like this:

The owner of a bar opened at 6 a.m. to serve persons waiting inside the bar for a 6:30 bus. He had a good bartender on this early shift, one who had developed quite a following. The owner felt, however, that his profits weren't up to what they should be. To get to the bottom of it, the owner came in early one morning and hid in the back room, where he could see the cash register and the bartender.

An early customer ordered Budweiser, placed a $5 bill on the bar, and started to sip his drink. Before he could get change, the customer saw the bus coming and decided to run out, leaving his Bud and five spot on the bar. As the bartender picked up the money and approached the cash register, he saw no one else in the vicinity. In a moment, the bartender turned away and slipped the five into his pocket.

Immediately, the owner stepped out of the back room, saying to his employee, "What's the matter, aren't we splitting it any more?"

CHAPTER 57

Drinking on the Job

Anheuser-Busch has always felt that quality brewing would be affected unless the company paid very close attention to all facets of the beer business.

Fine ingredients, such as pure water, imported hops, barley malt and rice, as well as proper aging and the use of beechwood chips, wouldn't mean much if a breakdown in cleanliness occurred at any phase of the brewing and product placement process, whether in packaging, storage, delivery or in actual serving of "The King of Beers."

The chapter on Mike Shagg and its reference to the merchandise school touched on the importance of consistency in the Anheuser-Busch brewing process.

The fact is that, with all of the attention given to our products, "serving" is obviously one of the most important steps. For that reason, the correct pouring of our premium brew into properly washed and drained glasses has always been a must. (Note that glasses should be washed thoroughly, not mixed with other utensils, and then allowed to drain dry. Never should beer glasses be dried with a towel or cloth.) This is always stressed in the merchandising school. And the advice is passed on from drummer to retailer with the hope that the consumer will become aware of it too.

To each his own, of course, but some people prefer to drink their Bud directly from the bottle or can, thereby missing the maximum enjoyment achieved when it is consumed from a "beer clean" glass. The proof is in the taste!

Now no drummer is required to overdo the tasting. But he is expected to try the Bud, to be alert to how cold it is, and to check the date on the package. Where Anheuser-Busch draft is sampled, attention is directed not only to temperature, but to pressure as well.

Bob Martin, mentioned several times in this book, was among the best drummers in the business.

On a specific day, Bob made his 12 calls on bars and restaurants in the downtown area. On that same day, Jerry Walsh and Mike Shagg made a series of calls on St. Louis retailers, including three in Bob's territory.

On the following morning, we all attended a sales meeting in Jerry's office, just as we did every month or so. Among the questions asked by Mr. Walsh was one addressed to Bob, regarding the previous day's activities.

"Bob, did you call on Bill Murphy's yesterday?"

Bob, always honest and to the point, responded, "Yes, sir, I did."

Walsh countered with, "Did you taste the beer?"

Martin answered, "No, sir, I didn't. It was 8:15 a.m., and I just had breakfast, that's all."

Jerry Walsh came as close to anger as I had ever seen him—and he dedicated the remainder of this meeting to the importance of "tasting the Bud" in *every* outlet, regardless of the hour of the day. After making his point, Jerry mellowed a little and regained his composure. With his familiar smile, he then adjourned the meeting.

As we all exited the office, Bob whispered to me, "How about that. I'm probably the only guy in the country who was almost fired for *not* drinking on the job!"

Teaching School

I suppose I attended the merchandising school dozens of times, both as a student along with other drummers from City Sales, and as the host in a program designed to inform retailers. The instructors were generally sales veterans who were able to bring their street experience to the classroom.

I was completely surprised one afternoon when I called my office and was told to report to George Renard in the Merchandising School. When I arrived about 4 p.m., George told me that one of his instructors was being promoted to district manager in Florida. If I were interested, he would like me to join his staff in the school. Now I was really surprised.

Bob Martin, who was leaving to take the promotion in Florida, was my good friend. So I wanted to talk with him before I made a decision. Bob encouraged me to accept the job. Certainly, it had been a wise step for him.

I recalled that Bill Bien, our national sales manager, had asked me on several occasions, during my time in a St. Louis territory, when I planned to go into the field "where the opportunities are." I felt that if a stint in the school as a prelude to field work had been a good plan for Bob, it might be for me as well. I accepted the offer and became an instructor in the school. My new home would be on the second floor of the Bevo plant in St. Louis.

This was a new life, but it was fun. Each week, we received a new class of employees or of wholesalers and their people. Most of them were knowledgeable in the beer business and anxious to share ideas.

For nine months, we conducted classes. During the summer we went into the field to work with wholesalers, where we could put into practice what we preached. The next step for me was an opportunity to travel year-round, just as I did during summer months. This time I specialized in the selling and merchandising of Busch Bavarian, our new popular brand.

In my new job, I traveled half of the country, one week in each market. In this role, I worked with wholesalers and their people to suggest the most effective ways of marketing our newest product. After introducing Busch Bavarian in the Tampa-St. Petersburg area of Florida, I was assigned to the state of Kansas. My first stop was Kansas City.

CHAPTER 59

The Wholesaler

One of the first things I learned when I joined An-heuser-Busch was the importance of the wholesaler and how many people were interested in becoming one.

The wholesaler (sometimes called the distributor) is a private business person who is authorized to represent the brewer in the sales, distribution and promotion of An-heuser-Busch products in a specified geographical area. This could be a county or an entire city, depending upon the territory's population and business potential.

I had the pleasure of meeting and sometimes working with many of the 500 or more wholesalers in the country, some of whom worked for the brewery previously. These

people had invested their money and hard work into ware-
housing, trucks and manpower (and, in many cases, accounts receivable), with no guarantee of an easy road. Some
have been fabulously successful, while others have just
"made a living." I mention this because of another thing I
learned: "It isn't easy."

The fine reputation of the brewer gives the wholesaler
a great gateway into the community. But in the end, it is his
dedication and hard work, plus his willingness to use the
expert advice and support offered by the brewery, that usually determines how successful he will be. Brewery representatives are always available to point out where ideas in
other markets have worked and how they might be just as
successful again. The advice is free, but the wholesaler de-
cides whether or not to act on it. The message is clear again:
running a successful business isn't so easy as many believe.
A smart wholesaler and the brewery both realize that each
plays an important role in a successful operation.

CHAPTER 60

Wholesaler High Jinks

Despite all the hard work involved in running a wholesale beer operation—loading and unloading trucks, checking inventories, and in special instances actually driving a truck—there is also a fun side to the business.

When civic, business or charitable organizations plan their meetings, conventions and other gatherings, they very often look for an interesting speaker. Naturally, they're seeking knowledgeable, entertaining men and women. Bud wholesalers are often just what the doctor ordered.

Later in my career, after actually joining an Anheuser-Busch wholesaler's operation, I made myself available and regularly appeared at breakfasts, lunches and dinners, always willing to deliver humorous stories, but carefully blended with the Budweiser message. And along with many other like-minded wholesalers across the country, I saw our program pay off.

The jokes aside, however, it was far more important that wholesalers answer the many questions about our product, talking in plain language about that most interesting of subjects, Budweiser.

As mentioned earlier, many of the questions we received were repeated meeting after meeting, so we were able to answer with ease and authority. Sometimes dispelling rumors became the prime task.

The hottest question, particularly among the "over 40" crowd, was often about Bock Beer. When oldtimers wanted a "spring tonic," for example, they used to take it in pleasant form—Bock Beer. More than a few questioners stoutly insisted that Bock Beer was actually brewed from the dregs of brewery barrels, and this misconception probably contributed to the great decline in popularity of Bock Beer each spring.

In truth, Bock Beer is not the dregs from a brewing process in any sense. It quite simply is made from a special recipe or formula, which gives the beer an unusual taste.

Unlike lecturers in some other fields, a speaker in the beer business has information that people on the street want. They will listen, ask questions, and discuss the subject with friends and family. No speaker, with the possible exception of sports, entertainment or high-ranking political figures, enjoys such an atmosphere in which to work a crowd.

So the next time you have a chance to hear your Budweiser wholesaler talk about the beer business, gather your questions, hurry to the meeting, get a good seat—and enjoy yourself!

Dick Wall merchandising Busch Bavarian Beer.

Joe Loriaux

There are several ways that a person can become a wholesaler. Sometimes it occurs through a family inheritance. Other times an experienced beer man already in the market receives an opportunity to take on Anheuser-Busch products. And occasionally, someone working for the parent company gets a chance to join an existing wholesaler.

While working as an instructor in the merchandising school, I became acquainted with some truly outstanding people. One of the most noteworthy was Joe Loriaux, owner of Superior Sales, the Bud and Busch wholesaler in Kansas City, Kansas. Although some very talented wholesalers came through the school, Joe Loriaux stood out among all of them.

I visited Joe's market late in 1958 as part of the brewery program designed to help wholesalers merchandise the new companion beer, Busch Bavarian. Joe and I became better acquainted. I met his lovely wife, Pat, and their two children, Peter and Janie. Spending time with Joe was always fun, but meeting his family was icing on the cake.

After some time, Joe mentioned in conversation that he was thinking about improving his business by adding a sales manager. After much thought and consideration of what a pleasant position I had at the moment, and then comparing my travel schedule with a chance to be home with my family at night, I finally asked Joe to consider me for the newly created post. Without hesitation, Joe hired me, and in a few months I had bought a home in Kansas. We moved to the Wheat State in April of 1959. I can't express what the change meant to us, and again Joe proved daily what a classy gentleman he is.

Working as sales manager at Superior Sales was in some sense routine, because I had duties virtually identical to those of sales managers in every Budweiser beer establishment in the country, whether wholesale or a branch.

Most of the drivers were aware of what they were expected to do. But subtle reminders never hurt. Occasional, brief meetings were not the most exciting part of a deliveryman's week, but Joe and I could see what an improvement they brought to our operation.

Rotation of the beer, while important, was seldom a problem in our single-county market. Two or three calls on a retailer each week allowed the driver to keep a close tab on inventory. Our people also soon realized that outside signs, billboards and point-of-sale merchandising materials within outlets really helped sell Bud and other Busch products. These few things, plus some of the tasks our driver/salesmen had performed for years, allowed us to boast of a particularly effective team.

Of course, both Joe and I made personal calls on retailers, sometimes inviting patrons to sample our Bud. We always remained constantly on the alert for spots where merchandising signs would improve our sales position.

Cultivation of friendships with grocery managers was a must. They usually had authority to allow the setup of special selling displays in their stores. Joe and I would actually do the stacking of six-packs of our beer, either at the end of a gondola or in some other high traffic location. This was always done in an attractive style so that consumers would find Bud or Busch accessible—and easy to slip into their shopping carts. This, of course, meant increased sales for the store, and a larger order when our driver/salesman made his next call.

There were many other details. Joe ordered beer from the brewery in St. Louis, while our personable office manager, Ruth Young, supervised the loading and unloading of trucks. She also handled the money from drivers at the end of the day, as part of the dozens of other duties which she performed. Ruth really kept the business rolling, allowing Joe and me to have time to do what we truly enjoyed—sell! I guess Ruth and I were both impressed by Joe. Along with his ownership of Superior Sales and other business interests, Joe never failed to pitch in on any occasion where he could help, including the loading or unloading of trucks and railroad cars.

Shortly after I joined Superior Sales, Joe took me to lunch for a business meeting at the Town House Hotel where we could discuss plans for improving our operation. His first question, as we sipped a pre-lunch Bud, was, "Which would you prefer, membership in a country club or in the Kansas City Advertising and Sales Executive Club? You have your choice, and Superior will pay the initiation fees and monthly dues!" I was completely surprised and told him so. He told me to think about it and talk it over with my wife, Mary Ellen.

Neither Mary Ellen nor I were into golf. So I decided to go for the Ad Club. Within two weeks I became a member at 913 Baltimore in Kansas City, Missouri. The club had several hundred members, owned its own building, and served both lunch and dinner daily, with bar and lounge available, operating much as one would have expected in the days of Sherlock Holmes. There were private meeting rooms and, on the second floor, a huge ballroom. In this room, a weekly meeting of members was held. We were able to invite guests for lunch and to hear top speakers. Among many, perhaps the best known were future President Ronald Reagan, National Speakers Association giant Bill Gove and actor Clint Eastwood.

These luncheons were for many years held on Wednesdays. We later moved them to Mondays to assure better attendance. The crowds increased, approaching 300 men and women each week. Circular tables for eight filled the room. And it gave members a chance to lunch with different people each week.

As a rule, I sat with brewery people who worked in advertising. Tables hosting advertising people also drew media people. Soon I had met many representatives from all the radio and TV stations, and I enjoyed comparing our varied radio experiences. One of the nicest persons I met was Clarence Brazeal, the administrative manager of KCMO Broadcasting. His title meant that he was not necessarily a "media man," but served instead as "the keeper of the purse strings" for KCMO. He answered only to the general manager, Joe Hartenbower.

Throughout that first year, I met many members. Not only by way of luncheons, but also through membership on entertainment committees, organizing holiday parties, and so on. Even some who didn't recall my name remembered me as the "Beer Baron." So both Bud and I were recognized. However, my work with Joe Loriaux came first, and business was good.

One of the things I had dabbled with while living in St. Louis was public speaking. That included appearances before civic clubs and other organizations at luncheons, dinners or regular meeting sessions. I say "dabbled" because it was certainly on a limited basis. But Joe encouraged me. He even used his influence to have me named as the featured speaker at a Kansas Beer Distributors convention. This led to appearances at many national conventions, as well as at all of the local civic clubs. Some of my appearances were as a serious speaker, and some as a humorist. This activity later culminated in membership for me in the National Speakers Association.

CHAPTER 62

A Good Beer Man

Perhaps the greatest compliment that one drummer can pay to another is that, "He's a good beer man." That term generally applies to a colleague who commands respect among those who work with him every day, both in the brewery family and also among retailers and consumers. But it is an especially high tribute when applied to a drummer who works for a competitor. And this situation perfectly describes Vic LaPorta, one of the outstanding beer drummers of all time.

Although I never met Vic until moving to Kansas City in 1959, his reputation in the beer industry was legendary. A native of Chicago, Vic came to Kansas City, where he represented "Schultz" Beer as the district manager for the Kansas and Missouri areas. He was a formidable competitor, to say the least. One of the best things to happen for Superior Sales, the Anheuser-Busch wholesaler in Kansas City, was Vic's decision to retire from the beer business. Vic had tired of the constant travel and wanted to spend more time with his beautiful family.

Vic found the perfect field in which to apply his considerable interpersonal and business skills, which he had developed over many years as a beer drummer—the insurance industry!

One reason Vic had enjoyed such success as a drummer was his love of people and the evident way he cared about them. Nobody has ever been better at remembering names and maintaining friendships, even among his strongest competitors. (As an example, Vic and I have enjoyed breakfast together every Friday morning for the last 30 years.) "Service" was always Vic's middle name, and "helping others" his long suit.

Vic received an opportunity to apply these concepts in the insurance industry when he accepted a position with the New England Mutual Life Insurance Company, where his ability to meet people, solve their problems, and help their families allowed him to develop an entirely new and highly successful career. This new career required very little travel, so that Vic could enjoy time with his wonderful family. Vic's wife, the beautiful Katherine Cassato LaPorta, gave him three fine sons and a splendid home environment in which to rear them.

Vic and Katherine are very special people. Mary Ellen and I are proud to count them among our very closest friends.

CHAPTER 63

The Barber of Civility

Most people would not associate opera with a barber-shop. Hirsute gentlemen in Kansas City, however, can enjoy a Mozart aria along with a haircut, courtesy of my good friend, Dan Tomaszczuk.

Dan is not your ordinary barber. He is well known in Kansas City for his tonsorial skills, and he counts among his customers some of Kansas City's most influential citizens. The thing that really sets him apart, however, is his truly outstanding singing voice. For more than 30 years now, I have enjoyed Dan's singing along with a shave and haircut.

Dan's musical talent has earned him recognition throughout the city, and our local newspapers and television stations have made him the subject of articles and stories about his "operatic" haircuts.

Dan developed his love for music in Ukraine, where he was born and lived until the end of World War II. After suffering first under communism, then under Nazi invaders, and finally under communism again, Dan finally emigrated from his homeland and eventually made his way to Kansas City, where he is recognized as one of its finest (and certainly the most musical!) barbers. His wife, Eleonore, recently became a citizen, and together they reared two sons, both of whom are quite successful in their chosen professions.

Dan has been both barber and good friend to me for more than a quarter century. May his rich baritone be with us for many years to come!

CHAPTER 64

A Tailor's Life

Perhaps the most valid test of a person's character is his attitude toward people after he himself has suffered great injustice at the hands of his fellow man. Jack Mittelman passes that test with flying colors.

I first met Jack Mittelman not long after moving to Prairie Village in 1959. Jack lives around the corner, and he has a tailor shop just a few minutes away. But there is more to Jack's story than being one of the world's finest tailors. He did not always lead the comfortable, suburban life of a successful businessman.

Jack's story began half a world away, in the Poland of pre-war Europe. The son of a tailor in the village of Pilica,

Jack was born in 1921. He worked as a boy at his father's side, learning "old world" European tailoring the way it had traditionally been done, as the apprentice to a master. It was in his father's shop that Jack learned the importance of quality tailoring, honesty and cheerful service to his customer. And it was there that he also developed the hallmarks of good character, such as perseverance, hard work and the spiritual strength that would carry him through an adversity that crushed weaker men.

Jack's life in Pilica was hard but good in those years leading up to World War II. The life he knew, however, was swept away in the wake of blood and death that accompanied Hitler's Nazi invasion of Poland. Though innocent like his brother Jews of any wrongdoing, Jack was arrested and thrown into a succession of horrific concentration camps. For the next five years, he was starved, beaten, and subjected to the cruelest regimen of slave labor.

By the war's end, Jack Mittelman had passed through a hell beyond even Dante's imagination. Jack was little more than a skeleton, and he had lost home, family and a way of life that would never return. Lesser men might have become embittered misanthropes. Jack, though, refused to allow Nazi tyranny and cruelty to crush his spirit. He rose above his tragic circumstances and immigrated to the United States. Jack soon began a new life in Kansas City, where he married his beautiful wife, reared two lovely daughters, and used his outstanding skills as a tailor to build a successful business.

Today, Jack continues his work in the tailoring field, where he is recognized as one of the world's best, and he continues to be a kind, generous and wonderful friend to all who know him. I am privileged to have Jack Mittelman as my tailor but, more importantly, to count him as one of my very dearest friends.

It's Kinda
Like the Fella Said

Show Business

For as many years as I can remember, I have had a love affair with show business and the people in it. Perhaps that's evident throughout this book. The truth is that the people I enjoy most are in the business of entertaining audiences for a living.

There is something fascinating about most of the men and women who choose this line of work. The singer isn't always warbling, the musician isn't always blowing his horn, nor is the actor always quoting from Shakespeare. But most of them are interesting persons, even when they aren't performing.

Just listening to a group of these people discussing their experiences can be very exciting. One story always leads to a more interesting one, and often show business is noticeably absent.

I recall sipping coffee with the famous band leader, Artie Shaw, and one of America's great trumpet players, Max Kaminsky, during World War II. Artie headed up a Navy band formed to entertain troops. He, Max, and several other top-flight musicians who had joined the Navy were touring the Southwest Pacific area. Our meeting occurred at the American Red Cross Restaurant in Brisbane, Australia.

Artie assembled an outstanding group. In addition to Max, it included Claude Thornhill on piano, Sam Donahue on sax, and one of the world's finest drummers, Davey Tough. Many other crack musicians joined the talented clarinetist leader, who had a marvelous musical insight, enabling him to thrill the jazz world with such smash hit records as "Stardust" and "Begin the Beguine." He was a master.

While some of his sidemen didn't seem to understand Artie, to a man they applauded his ability. Yet, as I talked with him late that night in Brisbane, I was amazed at his knowledge, not only of musical interpretation but of politics, world history and other topics as well. He was simply marvelous to encounter.

And yet he gave the impression that he felt he was talking over our heads in some areas, and perhaps he was. But his concern for details and understanding the other person made him a delightful conversationalist. We talked for two hours. And when he departed, I was longing for more.

CHAPTER 66

Entertainers

One of the most entertaining personalities of the '40s, '50s and '60s was Jimmy Edmundson, from Atlanta, Georgia. Jimmy had a knack for spelling words backwards. For example, mention the word *house* and Jimmy would quickly spell *esuoh*, that is, *house* spelled backwards. And he could do it with words of five or 15 letters. It didn't matter.

He wisely attired himself in the traditional cap and gown, used a blackboard on stage, and gave himself the obvious moniker "Professor Backwards." He worked theatres and nightclubs all over the country and was a regular on the Ed Sullivan and Steve Allen television shows.

I met him many times when he visited St. Louis to appear at the Fox and Ambassador Theaters and at the Chase and Jefferson Hotels.

In addition to his ability to spell backwards, Jimmy had a great appreciation for money. He never felt he was "close with a buck," but he always acknowledged wanting to do everything as economically as possible.

One of his ploys in those days was to save money on long distance phone charges. When calling collect to his agent, Benny Halpin, in Chicago to learn the location of his next booking and what his pay would be, Jimmy devised a scheme to get his calls free. The plan called for Jimmy to use long distance to reach his agent's office. He called collect, asking for himself, Jimmy Edmundson, by name. The agent would tell the phone operator, "Mr. Edmundson is not in." The Professor would then ask where he could be reached, and Benny would say, "He can be reached next Friday, Saturday and Sunday at the Chase Hotel in St. Louis," (giving him the location of the next gig). Then, according to the plan, he would state that his room number at the Chase would be 850. This indicated his fee would be $850.

Jimmy told me he used this scam to perfection. Calling one day, he learned from agent Benny in Chicago that he could be reached September 15 through the 30th in Kansas City's Muehlebach Hotel, Room 1200. Always looking for the best deal, Jimmy then asked, "Do you think you could arrange to move him to Room 1500?"

CHAPTER 67

Theatres

St. Louis had always been proud of its neighborhood and downtown theatres. The Fox, Missouri, St. Louis and Shubert houses gave Grand Avenue from Lindell to Delmar its own Great White Way. Downtown at 7th and Locust stood the Ambassador, while the beautiful Loew's State flourished as a first-run house, brightening Washington Avenue between 7th and 8th Streets. All of these featured first-run films, and each at one time or another offered outstanding stage shows.

This "golden age" of St. Louis movie theatres occurred as vaudeville was fading from the scene—while the old Gaity and the Grand were struggling to stay alive. At Grand

and Olive was the Empress Theatre, which at one time featured stage shows and films but later switched to motion pictures only. The American featured "legitimate" theatre at 7th and Market, but even with such attractions as the Lunts, the Barrymores and Cornelia Otis Skinner, a combination of building demolitions and Hollywood determination forced their performances to move to the Shubert Theatre. Later, the Orpheum at 9th and St. Charles became the home of "legitimate" theatre. While this was going on, some 30 to 40 smaller houses were gaining popularity across the city.

Neighborhood theatres featured movies which had already received a "first run" downtown, or which were "B" films, westerns or serials that never reached the city's major houses. Every neighborhood had one. Imagine seeing two pictures, plus a short subject and newsreel, all for an admission charge of just 10 or 15 cents.

Meanwhile, back downtown, smart operators, such as the Skouras brothers, the Arthurs and others, saw the popularity of live entertainment increasing, and they were quick to latch on.

In those early days, the Ambassador had Ed Lowry, an excellent MC, on a permanent basis. Ed was a very fine young man with a smile and style that held the women of St. Louis spellbound. When Lowry sang or even only spoke, the audience "swooned," and that was long before anyone had ever heard of Frank Sinatra. Lowry introduced singers, musicians and dancers and had fans lined up all day, starting as early as 10 o'clock in the morning. They loved Ed Lowry. Eventually, however, tastes began to change, and the years marched on. Ed Lowry retired to the West Coast, where he worked in a few films. But no one ever replaced Ed in the hearts of St. Louisans.

Brook Johns was another favorite for many years. Big bands like Benny Goodman, Kay Kyser and Tommy Dorsey were hot properties, and every big band had popular recordings that guaranteed big audiences when they made special personal appearances. Often the musical organization included singers and a comedian, with the bandleader serving as MC. The attraction was offered to the theatre as a package and, for all practical purposes, the local operators simply provided the theatre.

Later the Ambassador went to a semi-national plan. They brought in a nationally known musical director, Paul Ashe, as a permanent orchestra conductor. He then staffed the pit with top local musicians and brought in such stars as Morey Amsterdam, Mabel Todd, George Byron and others. Most stars appeared for one week, though Byron stayed on as a permanent entertainer.

At Grand and Washington, the Fox leaned toward the national attractions, too—offering a first-run film with guest orchestra and vocalists such as Horace Heidt, Louis Armstrong, Jackie Heller, Kay Kyser and St. Louisan Harry Babbitt.

Summertime found the outdoor "Muny Opera" in Forest Park the leading theatre for thousands of St. Louisans who sought high quality entertainment in the form of light opera, musical comedy and drama. The shows were performed nightly by nationally known singers and dancers, all supported by one of the finest orchestras in the world.

Such shows as *Desert Song, Bitter Sweet, The Merry Widow* and *Show Boat* are among the hits that audiences

*Rehearsal for "Twentieth Century" at the Civic Theatre
in the Summer of 1939.*

*Dick Wall (in sunglasses at front of stage right) attending rehearsal
of "Twentieth Century" at the Civic Theatre in 1939.*

were able to enjoy under the stars. Allan Jones, Robert Shaeffer, Vivian Siegal and Cary Grant are some of those who appeared at the "Muny."

Indoors, and at a high amateur level, was the "Little Theatre" on Union Boulevard just off Delmar. Sometimes referred to as the St. Louis Community Theatre, it gave young writers and actors a chance to break into show business while working with a group of experienced performers under the talented director, Gordon Carter.

Probably only a few will remember the "Civic" theatre, which operated during the late '30s and early '40s. Many who were active in the Little Theatre during fall and winter months also followed Director Carter during the summer, where a "stock" company produced such outdoor shows as *Twentieth Century*. Hollywood stars such as Ian Keith joined a local cast, which consisted of men and women of both amateur and professional status, to form this "summer stock" company. The theatre was located near McKnight and Litzinger Roads in St. Louis County, where today there is no trace of the structure. But some of us remember it fondly.

CHAPTER 68

Bob Goddard

There were many imitators of the legendary Bob Goddard, who was a reporter at the *Globe-Democrat* for many years. Imitators, but none to really compare.

Bob had a deep interest in people and the entertainment industry. His daily column was a result of his visits to the nightclub area and of his conversations with persons who made up that scene. Having naturally spent a great deal of time on the phone, he never depended on rumors. He was quick to hit the street so he could write with assurance. The readers knew that his word was true. And one of the most important parts of Bob's dedication to his job was the help he gave newcomers to show business.

If he knew of a performer who was scheduled to open in one of the clubs or lounges in St. Louis, Bob would make it a point to review the act in his column. And if he was unable to make the gig personally, he would poll customers and operators for a consensus. If he couldn't write "good things," he would skip a comment altogether and instead try to reach the performer to offer advice on how he or she could improve. Bob liked people, and he loved his craft. Thousands of readers looked forward to his morning column. His untimely death caused a great loss to *Globe-Democrat* readers and to his many friends and admirers across the St. Louis metropolitan area.

Garry Moore

Any list of entertainers who helped brighten the St. Louis scene during its glory years just has to include Garry Moore. Not a St. Louis native, but with family ties here, this brash young talent took St. Louis by storm. To the disappointment of his uncle, a St. Louis dentist who proudly used his family name of Morfit, Garrison Morfit chose the stage name "Garry Moore."

It was the mid-30s when KWK brought the young man with a crew cut from Baltimore. Barely out of his teens, Garry left no doubt in the minds of all who met him that St. Louis was just step one on a road to the big time. Danny Seyforth, the production manager at KWK, convinced management that an early afternoon Monday-Friday slot was just made for Garry.

You may be familiar with the difference between a comic and a comedian. A comic says funny things. A comedian says things funny. While I didn't realize it at first, it soon became apparent that this young man was capable of going either way. He could do it all!

With a studio orchestra, several vocalists and Garry as host, the show took off. Not only did he think funny, he brought out the best from others in the studio. Singers Gene Babbit and the beautiful June Curran Burton found they could add "comedy" to their resumes, and listenership increased.

Garry made personal appearances, and the newspapers hailed him as a new star. As a result, KWK was riding high. KMOX, always the powerhouse in our St. Louis market, continued its lead, but KWK made inroads. There was one thing KWK couldn't control, however. Word of Garry's ability reached beyond the city—far beyond. Soon the talent we all enjoyed became more and more appreciated by the networks. It began when Ransom Sherman, host of "Club Matinee" on the NBC Network from Chicago, had some Hollywood commitments to fulfill. This caused NBC to look for a substitute. KWK allowed Garry to fill in occasionally. But they knew it was only a matter of time until a call would come, taking the young star to Chicago. The irony of all this was that Ransom Sherman, only a few years before, had hosted "The Laugh Clinic" on KMOX. And in the same fashion, he left for "Club Matinee" at NBC Chicago. Sherman himself later moved permanently to the West Coast, where he was quite successful.

After only a few years, Garry moved on and soon found himself in nighttime radio for CBS. Continuing the advance, CBS and Camel cigarettes placed Garry on a weekly radio show with the fabulous Jimmy Durante. This appeared to be a wise move. The barroom antics of Durante and the youthful sophistication of Garry Moore proved an unbeatable combination, and their show quickly became successful.

After only two or three seasons, Durante surrendered to the temptation of movies and television. Moore began to wing it, and Rexall, a relatively new radio sponsor, came to pick him up.

As the world moved on, radio stars were anxious to try television. Garry Moore was among the leaders. With his famous crew cut and a smile from ear to ear, plus that proven knack for making people laugh, one could almost argue that the medium and the star truly were made for each other.

The Garry Moore Show became an instant winner, bringing names like Carol Burnett, Durwood Kirby, Tim Conway and others into the homes of viewers all over the country. But this isn't a television review. It is simply a reminder of how a bright young man, who spent part of his life in our fair city, brightened the lives of many thousands of St. Louisans before moving on to prove the predictions of those exposed to his humor.

I shall never again sip a Budweiser in the Steeplechase of the Chase Hotel with this great talent. But it is a privilege and great pleasure to call on that memory from time to time.

CHAPTER 70

George Jessel

At the risk of sounding overly zealous in my analysis of entertainers, we can add to our list of classy guys the name of that internationally known after-dinner speaker, George Jessel. He was still a speaker when he died in 1981, and show people by the hundreds paid tribute to him. I believed his every word.

Here was a man who made it to the top of his profession in an era which produced Jack Benny, Eddie Cantor, Milton Berle, Bob Hope, George Burns and so many more. These people were dedicated to one purpose—making people laugh. Each had his own style and persona, to the extent that they were predictable. Jack Benny was a tightwad; Bob Hope was the wise guy trying to get a date. George Burns smoked his cigar and played straight man to his wife. Predictable, yes, but always funny. For if comedians weren't funny, they didn't last.

Jessel was unusual in that he began as a singer, songwriter and eulogist. His "shtick" was simply a telephone conversation with his mother. On the face of it, this doesn't seem to be very funny. But Jessel made it so. In fact, he became so proficient that, as vaudeville began to fade from the entertainment scene, Jessel grew stronger. Soon he was able to keep busy between radio and TV gigs with personal appearances as master of ceremonies or the featured speaker at breakfasts, luncheons or dinners all over the country.

Just knowing George Jessel was fun. But one of the brightest spots in my professional life was appearing on a program with him. The man President Franklin Roosevelt named "Toastmaster General of the United States" was the featured speaker at a national convention in Kansas City. Perhaps to inject local flavor, or perhaps to keep costs at a reasonable level (I was living in Kansas City at the time), I was offered the chance to appear before a national audience at this convention.

I delivered a humorous talk-with-a-message, but George absolutely fractured the audience with his material. Having followed his career since my childhood, I was very aware of his great talent. And you can be sure there was no chance of me upstaging him, or even trying. His place as the dinner speaker followed three hours after mine, but it was worth waiting for. He was a riot.

A few hours before my scheduled engagement, I called George to invite him for a drink. He was delighted and suggested that, because he would not be dining at the event, we could perhaps have dinner together later in the evening. I agreed to catch up with him after the banquet. We met and proceeded to the Terrace Grill of the Muehlebach Hotel, where the convention was housed. The maitre d' seated us at a table for two. I told Jessel that I had followed his career and was hoping to learn more about the speaking business. He seemed happy to oblige and appeared to relax as we sipped Budweiser and discussed the styles of some other professionals. He understood that I was relatively new to the speaking field, and he tried to help.

After an hour or so, the restaurant began to fill with people. Most of them were connected with the convention. Before long, requests for Jessel's autograph were evident. As 15-20 persons formed a line at our table, I sat back and admired the star. Needless to say, I was surprised when, after each signature on napkins, menus or note paper, George thanked the fan and passed the pen to me, saying to the man or woman, "Here, I know you want Dick Wall's autograph, too. It will be nice to have some day."

From those few autographs I signed, I received two more invitations to speak nationally, the start of a wonderful career as a public speaker. Any wonder that George Jessel is on my list of "Classy Guys"?

CHAPTER 71

Davey Bold

Davey Bold was another entertainer with whom I spent a lot of time. Our friendship began during the early days in St. Louis when he played the old Claridge Hotel at 18th and Locust. We stayed in close touch through the Vegas days, where he appeared with Rowan and Martin and other stars, until he settled in Omaha. From there, he commuted to gigs all over the nation.

Davey was unusual. He had a love for show business second only to his family. His wife, Louise, and daughter, Candy, were so important to him. While he enjoyed the business immensely, he loved to talk about them.

Davey Bold

I always thought Davey was one of the most talented people I'd ever known. He played fine piano, sang, and joked with the audience as no one else could do. I know there was Fat Jack Leonard and, of course, Don Rickles. But no one combined the three Bold ingredients as he could. Davey Bold possessed a comedic mind second to none.

My good friend Davey Bold suffered a massive heart attack and died on July 18, 1978, in Omaha, Nebraska.

On the night of his burial, as a tribute to this talented man, operators of Omaha restaurants and nightclubs throughout the entertainment district dimmed their lights for two minutes, an action never known before or since in the adopted hometown of Davey Bold.

CHAPTER 72

Tony DiPardo

To list Tony DiPardo among our favorite entertainers is perhaps an understatement. Tony has excited so many, and been so good for so long, that he has to be a super personality.

Born in St. Louis in 1912, he became interested in music at a very early age. He started playing the trumpet at the age of six. By 13 years old, he was playing with the big guys. After joining the musicians' union, he was heard by big-name bandleader, Joe Reichman, who invited Tony to join his group and go on the road.

During ten years with the "Poet of the Piano," Tony played for dancers and listeners from the Mark Hopkins in

San Francisco to the Plaza Hotel in New York, and most points in between. The Reichman band was a draw wherever it played, a guaranteed moneymaker in hotels and nightclubs across the country. After a decade with Reichman, however, Tony developed a burning desire to head his own band and test his own ideas.

As the man fronting his own band, Tony finally had a chance to be himself. Strutting across the stage with his trusty, sweet-sounding trumpet and a top hat, Tony often made people forget Ted Lewis. But more importantly, he played music designed for dancing and listening. His audiences loved it. And they loved him.

In 1939, the young band leader moved into the Boulevard Room of the old Jefferson Hotel in St. Louis, where he packed the house for more than a year. By this time, even those who had never before heard of Tony DiPardo grew to love him as an entertainer.

Unlike some in the business, Tony really knew how to entertain. Throughout the '30s and '40s under his direction and management, the band played what people in all parts of the country wanted to hear. They saw Tony and a group of personally selected young musicians who really wanted to be at their best.

I knew Tony from the early days, when I was trying to break into St. Louis radio. He was playing the Forest Park Highlands, the Arcadia Ballroom and many other spots where dancers gathered. St. Louis loved his music, his wide smile and overall charm.

Tony's popularity stemmed from many sources, not the least of which was his ability to select talented people as his sidemen. He knew music, and he established a style that others couldn't duplicate.

Word of this musical package began to spread, and soon the band was traveling throughout the Midwest, including Kansas City. This town, famous for its jazz and blues, was captivated by a different type of music when Tony opened at the nationally known Muehlebach Hotel in 1940.

Tony had been asked by his agent where he would like to be booked. And with the entire country to choose from, Tony named Kansas City—the first choice of most bandleaders at that time. The attraction? Nightly coast-to-coast broadcasts from an outstanding first-class hotel!

Every orchestra featured a girl vocalist, and Betty Ellis came from St. Louis to be part of the DiPardo organization. Betty had a boyfriend in St. Louis. She wanted to marry the fellow, but for one reason or another, he had managed to avoid the marriage scene.

When Betty came to Kansas City, the boyfriend called to say that, if she would come off the road and return to St. Louis, he would take her down the aisle. Betty gave notice, and Tony was in the market for a singer. The rest of this story on his search for a replacement was told to me years later by Tony himself.

Barney Allis, the Muehlebach Hotel general manager, suggested that he call a very talented young radio singer whose name was Ann Ryan. Barney thought she might be just what Tony was seeking. Tony heard the girl and offered her a job. He then learned she really was a "young" girl—17 years old, to be exact. When Tony asked if she could travel and "go on the road," she told him that he would have to come to her home and meet her mother. And so he did!

Tony learned then that Ann Ryan was a stage name. Her real name was Madora Cropper, and her mom called her "Doddie." Mom approved, and Ann Ryan joined the DiPardo band.

Mom made the first road trip with her daughter and the band, but she didn't have to take too many trips thereafter: one year later, Tony and his beautiful young vocalist were married.

When I visited Kansas City in the late '50s, a colleague and I were strolling along Baltimore Avenue looking for a nightclub show. To my great surprise, there on the marquee outside the famous Eddy's on 13th Street was the name in lights: "Tony DiPardo and His Band." And under that, with second billing, was the name of Jerry Vale.

"Mr. Music"
Tony DiPardo

I hadn't talked to Tony since our days in St. Louis. So after seeing the show, in which he was really the star, I learned that he had been playing Kansas City with his band for quite some time. After a stint by Tony at the Eddy nightspot, its owners offered him an opportunity to head up the house band. The Eddy brothers are great judges of talent. Again, his personally selected musicians served as backup for Tony's special style. This style lent an additional professional touch to visiting acts, including Steve and Eydie, Sammy Davis, Jr., Andy Williams and others. The truth is that the Eddys were able to bring in big names because the word from entertainers coast to coast was that "working Kansas City is one of the most enjoyable gigs because you work with Tony DiPardo." They all wanted to work Eddy's in Kansas City. Tony brought houses packed with local fans, tourists and traveling businessmen.

As downtown Kansas City changed, so did the nightclub business. But Tony was able to adjust. He opened "Tony's Party House," where dances, wedding parties, banquets and public or private functions kept him busier than he really wanted to be.

When Kansas City was granted a pro football franchise, owner Lamar Hunt introduced Tony again, this time as the Kansas City Chiefs' director of music. With a much larger band, Tony not only excited thousands of fans as they entered the stadium for Sunday games, but he kept the fever at a high pitch throughout the contest.

The world has changed. The nightclub and big band picture is not what it once was, but Tony DiPardo goes on. Now in his 80s, you'll find him at the Chiefs games, or at most of the social functions in Kansas City. Tony points proudly to his lifetime as an entertainer, to his 25-year association with the Kansas City Chiefs and to his reputation among his peers. But his real pride lies in the beautiful family his lovely bride of more than 50 years has given him. That family is best described as musical. Daughter Patty has made her own way as a beautiful and very talented songstress fronting her own band. And in the sports business, Patty serves as assistant to her dad, who now continues to be director of music for the Chiefs, while continuing to work with his own band.

And Tony DiPardo is still known in Kansas City as "Mr. Music."

CHAPTER 73

Oscar Info

Most of us who are movie buffs are familiar with the "Oscars." These awards are given to those actors, directors, producers and others who, in the judgment of a majority of the thousands of members of the Academy of Motion Picture Arts and Sciences, have been the best in their field that year.

From the name Oscar came Emmy, Grammy, Tony and other titles in various media. But why the name "Oscar"?

After winning the Academy award for Best Actress in 1935, Bette Davis and her husband, Harmon O. Nelson, Jr., joined other Hollywood movie people in a series of parties and social functions following the awards banquet.

The early morning hours following that evening of glory found Bette and her partner unwinding with a nightcap in the living room of their home. Bette had placed the statue, which symbolized her ascendancy to the peak of the cinematic arts, on a mantle over the fireplace. As they raised a toast, each wondered why no one had ever named the symbol. "Let's give him a name," Bette said. As they raised their glasses, in an almost frivolous moment, she shouted, "Let's drink to us and to Harmon 'Oscar' Nelson, Jr.—that's it, we'll name him after you—we'll call him 'Oscar.'"

Soon after, the word *Oscar* was heard around Hollywood. And when columnists like Hedda Hopper and Jimmie Fiddler picked it up, the name went international. Yes, you guessed it, Harmon O. Nelson, Jr., is the same man mentioned and pictured elsewhere in this book, the man who gave me such support and who became such a good friend.

CHAPTER 74

Winning One for the Gipper

Like so many soldiers during World War II, I was assigned to the famous "Cow Palace" in San Francisco while
waiting to depart for duty overseas. It happened to thousands of other GIs, and it happened to me.

With only a few days to spend in this California staging area, our most important concern was simply to keep
busy. So when we heard that movie stars Ronald Reagan
and Jeanette McDonald had arrived to greet and entertain
us, lines began to form several hours before showtime.

The stars had their own admirers. Most of us had seen
Miss McDonald in those great musicals with the talented
baritone, Nelson Eddy. Reagan, of course, had appeared in

many movies following his career as a sportscaster. He was probably best known at that time for the 1940 Pat O'Brien movie *Knute Rockne, All-American,* where he played the legendary George Gipp (who in the words of Rockne himself was "the first All American named by Walter Camp at Our Lady's School").

In order to ease crowd congestion at the pre-show autograph session, Army officials had situated the stars about 200 feet apart behind a belt-high, chain-link fence so that the lines could flow smoothly. From those vantage points, each star could shake hands, sign autographs, and answer questions.

Shortly before showtime, the audience (as did most audiences at that time) called out, "Win one for the Gipper," as soon as Reagan appeared near the stage. I got into the line leading to Ronald Reagan, who wore the uniform and insignia of a cavalry second lieutenant. I knew something of his background as a sportscaster in Des Moines and Davenport, Iowa, before he moved to Hollywood.

As I waited my turn to shake hands, I tried to think of something to say other than the trite, "I always enjoy your films, sir." I remembered that, in those days, there was a great sports bar and steakhouse in Des Moines called "Pinky's," which I had visited on occasion. I knew, of course, that Ronald "Dutch" Reagan was a regular there when he worked for radio station WHO.

As Lt. Reagan finished signing an autograph for the fellow ahead of me, I called out, "What do you hear from Pinky's?" Lt. Reagan stopped, took off his glasses (he never permitted photographs when he had them on), and smiled at me.

"Do you know Pinky?" he asked, with more than a hint of surprise in his voice.

I felt I had pressed the right button, because he leaned forward and shook my hand like I was a long-lost friend. I explained that I was a sports announcer from the Midwest, and then I made some reference to things he had done and to the "Dutch" moniker he had used on the air during his pre-Hollywood days. Although others in line were eager to meet him, the star asked me to stay with him. He continued to greet others but kept our conversation going as well. We talked about Iowa, St. Louis, the Midwest, and sports broadcasting in general for more than ten minutes. As showtime approached, a captain came along to bring the reception line to an end. He was obviously concerned with getting the concert underway.

As the officers started toward the stage, Dutch motioned for me to come along, and he kept our conversation going. When he ascended the ten or so steps to stage level, he introduced me to Miss McDonald. What a thrill!

With several thousand GIs waiting out front and clapping to hear the concert, our captain talked to Lt. Reagan about the opening spot and other details. It was obvious from their conversation that the captian had never handled an entertainment detail before. As their discussion continued, the audience was getting impatient, and the performers were at last ready, though I wasn't part of the act.

When someone asked who would introduce Reagan, Dutch surprised everyone by saying, "Here's an old sportscaster who's headed overseas in a few days, and I think he can handle a little intro. Hey, Dick, you want to take a crack at it?"

When he asked, I couldn't help but feel a bit sorry for the captain. It was evident that our captain assumed he would introduce Reagan. Even though this involved only introducing our famous guest and not serving as MC, I'm sure the captain felt his rank should have carried some weight. I didn't hesitate, though. With about two minutes' notice, I grabbed a mike and did the job. I didn't dwell but just kept it simple.

When I thanked Dutch after the concert, he simply broke into that winning smile and said, "Well, that's just one sportscaster to another!"

Some years later, while a member of the Kansas City Advertising and Sales Executives Club, I enjoyed visiting with Dutch Reagan again, when he talked to our membership as part of his work as a spokesman for General Electric. We had a good chuckle reminiscing about our wartime radio and entertainment experiences.

In San Francisco and in Kansas City, we all knew who Ronald Reagan was. None of us realized what he would become.

CHAPTER 75

Make Room for Daddy

One of the truly great comedic talents of the twentieth century was Danny Thomas. I had the pleasure of spending some time with him in Lake Tahoe, and I was privileged to witness the warm, human side of this kind and generous man.

Danny's career is probably well known to older people. Born Amos Jacobs, Danny changed his name. Why? Because he believed that "Danny Thomas" looked better in lights. For years since the 1930s, he tickled the funny bones of nightclub patrons across the country. When television arrived, he came right into their homes. The quintessential "family entertainer," Danny always "worked clean." As a result, he was loved by audiences throughout the world.

Though highly paid as an entertainer, Danny never turned down an opportunity to appear at a benefit. He was especially active in raising funds for St. Jude's Children's Hospital in Memphis. Through his efforts and those of his family and friends, many millions of dollars flowed into this worthy charitable institution.

Although I had never met Danny Thomas during my St. Louis days, I had seen him entertain hundreds of people in the Chase Hotel back in the '30s. Like so many others, I was won over completely by Danny's charm and sense of humor.

In the summer of 1967, Mary Ellen and I gathered up our teenage sons and headed for a vacation in California. We boarded a TWA flight for San Francisco, where we enjoyed two or three days in that beautiful "City by the Bay," and then cruised down Highway 1 toward Los Angeles. The entire family loved it.

Shortly after hitting the highway, we began to see billboards plugging various hotels and restaurants along the way. Most of them failed to elicit much interest. But then we saw it: "In Person—Danny Thomas—at Harrah's in Lake Tahoe." I wasn't sure how great a detour from our planned itinerary a visit to that famous resort would be, so we stopped at a nearby gas station for directions. We soon were back on the road, headed straight for Tahoe. I really wanted Mary Ellen and the boys to enjoy a performance by Danny Thomas.

I don't recall how many miles we traveled. Before long, however, we arrived at Harrah's, just in time for dinner. I was happy to learn that Danny would go on at 7:30, which gave us a little more than two hours for dinner. Mary Ellen and I ordered a couple of "Buds," while the boys enjoyed soft drinks.

During dinner, I assured the family that we were in for a delightful, funny show. The boys were eager to see it, and Terry, our youngest, wondered if we could meet the show's star. I told him we'd try.

Immediately after dinner, Mary Ellen said she'd rather relax at the table, so the boys and I headed backstage alone. I wasn't sure what to expect. But as we approached the dressing room, a very polite security guard came up to us. I told him that we wanted to meet Mr. Thomas. The guard at first explained that this would not be possible.

I mentioned that I was in the business and worked for a broadcast company that carried Mr. Thomas' shows. The guard paused for a moment, and then asked us to wait while he went in to confer with the star. After a few minutes, the security man emerged from the dressing room. He invited me in, but suggested that the boys rejoin Mrs. Wall at the table. I was disappointed, but the boys seemed to understand.

The dressing room turned out to be an apartment or bungalow, beautifully furnished and containing a wet bar, plus other amenities. It was a facility made available to the headliner of every Harrah's show. This month it was the home-away-from-home for Danny Thomas.

I can't begin to describe the warmth of this wonderful entertainer, and the thrill I experienced when I met and sat down with this fabulous comedy star. Danny was munching on a sandwich and sipping a Coke. He motioned for me to share the snacks, and we began to talk. During the first few minutes, I mentioned my sons, and Danny picked up on it right away.

"They're here at the show?" he asked.

When I told him they were, this lovable funny-man-with-a-big-heart insisted that they join us. He called the security man and asked him to visit my table and bring the boys in. While we waited, Danny and I continued to talk, mostly about comedy, television and personal appearances. He deplored the use of "blue material" by some comedians, emphasizing how important it was to remain dedicated to wholesome, family-oriented entertainment in order to be happy and successful.

"Look at the beautiful living quarters I'm given here," he said. "It's first class, but I'd rather be home with my family. This is the price we pay to be in the business and to make people laugh."

Danny then joked about hot dogs as his Sunday dinner. "It's not hot dogs every Sunday," he laughed, "but it does happen. God has been good to me, though. He's given me a happy home life, plus the ability to entertain people. I'm very blessed and very grateful."

As he spoke, our friendly guard brought the boys into Danny's dressing room. Their eyes practically popped out as they shook hands with Danny Thomas. He invited them to sit down and talk while sharing a hot dog and soft drink with this wonderful comedy star. It was heartwarming to see, and an experience my family will never forget.

When Danny Thomas died recently, I remembered our visit. And I joined an audience of millions in mourning the death of this great man and fabulous star of the comedic art. His goodness and charity will live on in happy memory, long after the laughter fades away.

CHAPTER 76

Music Is Still Alive

Much of my interest in music was put on hold while I was away from broadcasting. But it never really died.

My return to the world of broadcasting meant exposure to music by way of recordings and tapes during the day. But an opportunity to see more nightlife came with the nocturnal entertainment of clients and agency representatives.

Sure, Kansas City had a reputation from way back as the home of a very special type of jazz. Count Basie, Charlie Parker and others, for example, put us on the musical map, but slowly the picture changed.

Marilyn Maye and Kay Dennis brought a different though very exciting sound to Kansas City, and fans packed the restaurants, clubs and piano bars.

Peggy Clark sat at the keyboard, playing and singing to packed houses at Eddy's Le Boeuf in the Prom at 7th and Main. And later she teamed with banjoist Ted Painter for the same results at the Roaring '20s.

Dixieland, a form of jazz frowned upon by many purists, became a big item when the Red Onion Jazz Baby group played the Bristol on the Plaza.

Warren Durrett retired after a great career as the leader of a big band, and Steve Miller began to excite the town with his style, plus the great singing of Julie Turner. Later, Julie teamed with her husband and talented drummer, Tommy Ruskin, to perform wherever music lovers gathered.

Jazz pianist Mike Ning and song stylist Sherry Jones, another very talented husband and wife team, have made a great name for themselves all over the area, including Regan's Sunset Grill, where they have appeared for years.

Pianists usually lead, but those who can both play and sing are always in demand. Carolyn Abbott is particularly strong in that area. She has done it all, with an ability to adjust from jazz combo to sweet-sounding dance music. She's always fine.

And the ever popular Jim Murray, Dave McCubbin and so many more make it possible for natives and visitors to be assured of outstanding music at their fingertips. Jim, always dependable at the Holiday Inn, and Dave, who has played for years at Inge's, are just more proof that while music has changed, it has been for the better.

And so shall it always be.

Return
to a First Love

CHAPTER 77

KCMO Contact

One fall afternoon, I received a phone call from Sid Tremble, manager of KCMO-TV Channel 5 in Kansas City. He said he had talked with Clarence Brazeal about me and asked if I would be interested in visiting his station for a talk. I didn't have any details, but I made an appointment and arranged my work schedule to allow a visit to the television station.

Channel 5 was in a two-story building at 125 E. 31st Street, which also housed KCMO Radio, plus their FM station and the Muzak operation. Executive offices were on the second floor, with studios and program offices at street level. I identified myself at the reception desk and was asked to wait for a moment.

Down the stairs, to escort me to Tremble's office, came his attractive, well-dressed administrative assistant, Pat Bradley. As we walked up the stairs, I recall feeling that, while I didn't know much about the station, they certainly realized the importance of putting their best foot forward when they dispatched Pat to greet me.

Tremble welcomed me. As we sat down in his comfortable office, Sid assured me that he was a Budweiser drinker. For a little while, we talked beer and advertising.

After a few minutes, Tremble told me that they were planning to add a time salesman. He said Brazeal had mentioned that I might be considered for the position, if indeed I were interested. I told him I was both surprised and interested. As mentioned earlier, I had attempted to get into media sales back at WTMV but was unable to find an opportunity. I told him I would like to think about it for a few days. Before I left the station, Tremble introduced me to his television sales manager, Lee Marts.

Marts, a charming man with a beautiful speaking voice, greeted me warmly. His voice prompted me to remark that he could function as a television performer as well as a sales executive. He responded that he had indeed appeared as an actor. Lee was truly a person who found a field of employment outside the customary channel of his educational accomplishments. Marts held a degree in theatre, plus a law degree. In addition, he had risen to sales manager of a powerful television station. I was very impressed. After about 90 minutes, I departed the station. I left not with an offer of employment but with a positive feeling toward

Channel 5, based entirely on my contacts with Clarence Brazeal, Sid Tremble, Lee Marts and Pat Bradley.

I didn't mention my meeting to anyone because I didn't actually have an offer in hand. For that matter, I might never have one. So I thought and waited until Lee Marts called one day, inviting me to come over to his office.

I was prepared for anything, but the thought of being back in broadcasting really caused my heart to skip. Any concern I felt was eased when I reached the "Tall Tower." Marts was very candid. He said they were interested in me and had planned to train me on the studio set and in a control room before turning me loose as a salesman on the street. They changed their minds, however, because an experienced television salesman had become available. They were going with the other man.

I was disappointed but couldn't find fault. Experience won out. Lee Marts surprised me again when he asked, "Would you be interested in selling radio time?" I didn't hesitate. I said I would consider radio if it were offered.

Marts took me to meet Bill McReynolds, sales manager of KCMO Radio. Bill was a St. Louis native who graduated from the University of Missouri School of Journalism. After two years in Texas, he joined KCMO as a newscaster. At that time, air personnel at the Meredith stations worked in both TV and radio. Bill had finally moved into radio sales and ultimately became sales manager. He said he wanted to take on a new salesman, but had to get approval from general manager Joe Hartenbower. Bill was not successful in getting his subject on Hartenbower's agenda, so he said he wanted to keep in touch with me, which he did.

Bill and I had lunch frequently and had agreed on salary. But I still made special efforts to do quality work for Superior Sales, and beer sales were good. After six weeks without any indication that the KCMO general manager was any closer to a decision on an additional salesman, I made a trip to the sales manager's office. I told Bill that I should be dropped from consideration. The uncertainty of the situation might affect my concentration, which would be unfair to my present employer. Bill said he understood, and then apologized. With a friendly handshake, I departed.

About four weeks later, I received a call from Bill, who invited me to lunch at Putsch's 210 Restaurant on the Plaza. I agreed to meet him the following day. I really thought it would just be a friendly meeting of two ex-St. Louisans who simply wanted to "keep in touch." But I was pleasantly surprised.

As we sat at our table sipping a Budweiser in the posh eatery, Bill casually said, "Listen, I wanted to tell you that Hartenbower has given me the okay to hire you, if you're still interested in joining KCMO Radio." I smiled and said that I wanted to hear more. Bill went into details that we hadn't discussed before, such as some of the accounts I would be calling on, and how he felt I could contribute. Of course, we had discussed the salary and commission plan in earlier meetings, so I assumed the figures were unchanged.

Before I had a chance to accept his offer, Bill came up with an unusual suggestion. He said, "All of the points I have covered are firm. However, I hope you'll tell me that you will accept the offer, but only with an increase in the base pay we discussed." This brought a quick acceptance from me, although I knew my proposal would again have to go before E. K. Hartenbower. Since we really hadn't finalized our deal, my next step was to talk with Joe Loriaux, who was a great friend as well as the perfect employer.

While Bill McReynolds was talking with his top brass, I sat down with my friend Joe. I explained that I had not started out seeking a job, but that I had talked with KCMO, and then removed my name from their list, only to be contacted again by the station. Joe remarked that I had always possessed a great interest in broadcasting. He added that, if I left, there would be no hard feelings. The sincerity of Joe Loriaux was never more evident than when I confided in him that if indeed the KCMO deal worked out, I would have to take a physical exam. And I learned I might not pass as a result of "borderline diabetes."

Joe said, "If you want the job, take it. And if you flunk the physical, come back and be my sales manager." That's class!

Joe Hartenbower approved the deal, and it turned out that a physical wasn't necessary. I gave two weeks' notice, during which I performed my duties in the beer business. But I couldn't avoid glancing ahead at my return to radio.

CHAPTER 78

Return to Radio

I drove into the KCMO/Meredith parking lot near 31st and Main on a cold, snowy morning. I then climbed stairs to reach the station's radio sales office. Though many workers were delayed by the blizzard conditions, Bill McReynolds was there to welcome me. Joe Hartenbower had issued a memo to his staff noting my addition to the broadcasting team. As a result, many who had arrived on time approached me, identified themselves, and welcomed me aboard. The greetings continued through most of the morning, causing me to forget about the temperature outside. Personal introductions continued through most of the day.

George Stump was the radio program director. When we were introduced in his office, George recalled that we had met at a Kansas City, Kansas, Chamber of Commerce breakfast. As we shook hands, I realized that not only had we met, but his reputation was more familiar to me than the man himself. Anyone who had an interest in radio, and particularly music, had to have known George Stump. Born in Oklahoma and reared in Carthage, Missouri, where he started in radio, George moved into Kansas City broadcasting and established himself as a true authority on "Big Band" music. As a well-known disc jockey, George not only knew the music, but he knew the recording artists as well. And from the entertainment people I talked to, nobody in town had interviewed more "Show Biz" persons than he. Knowing that George was in charge of the program department and announcing staff helped me to realize what a quality product I would have.

In the next day or two, I met most of the announcers. Don Warnock, John Yates, Jim Gammon, Dick Guthrie, Ken Motley, Chuck Davis, Hugh Bowen, Jack Elliott and Jim Newman were some of the talented announcers who worked full time. One of the best set of pipes heard on Radio 810 belonged to a young man named Mike Shanin. He worked part time while in the Army in Kansas City, after first serving in Vietnam. Following discharge from service, Mike joined the announcing staff full time.

Music, sports and news made up our product, and I felt I was joining a crack sales staff. Clotis Barker from Mountain Grove, Missouri, was a skilled radio man when he joined KCMO. Jack Jester was another experienced announcer turned successful sales executive, while Joe Lugar was an advertising man from Kansas City, Kansas. All of them worked well under Bill McReynolds. The manager of the radio station was Dick Evans, whose dad, Tom Evans, founded the station. Dick was a genial leader who had a knack for meeting people and closing the deal. He would have made it to the top regardless of who founded the station.

The FM station was directed by Chris Stolfa and George Kieffer. Both were very talented and had a great reputation in the advertising community.

I've noted that Sid Tremble managed television while Lee Marts directed television sales. "Dutch" Meyers (whose wife, Jan Meyers, was later elected to the U. S. Congress, where she still serves), Glenn Walser, Don Johnson and Dick Walker also worked in sales.

The KCMO news department was headed by another "Mizzou" graduate, Harold Mack. He sounded great on the air but also directed the news activities on FM and TV 5.

Ken Coy, Dick Jamison, Wendall Anschutz, Lew Boles, Lou Cupp, Joe Kramer, Stan Cramer, Mike McGee and others made up a top quality on-the-air staff that was hard to match.

One of the most talented people was Jim Newman, a tall, handsome and athletic young man with the impeccable good manners of a true gentleman. Jim did news, TV weather, classical music and theatre reviews. Others soon recognized his enormous talent, which eventually led him from Kansas City to the network in New York—and then to Hollywood, where he has been a huge success.

Don Harrison, a TV anchor, also went to the national level and has for years been a key performer on CNN.

Sports was headed by nationally known Bruce Rice, who over the years was assisted by Merle Harmon, Monte Moore and Lynn Faris, all of whom were experienced national broadcasters, particularly in the area of major league baseball. KCMO was always first in sports in the Kansas City area.

A farm department directed by Paul Pippert and George Stephens saw farmers over many states turning to Radio 810 for the latest in agricultural news.

And no list of KCMO personalities would be complete without the name of perhaps the station's most effective communicator, Bill Yearout.

And no broadcasting facility could function as a market leader without a solid, knowledgeable engineering department. Led by chief engineer Carl Troeglin, dozens of technicians kept us on the air and enabled our broadcast team to produce quality sound—whether from studios, from remote locations, or in "feeds" to the CBS network. Vic Anderson, Bob Bowen, Don Thomas, Ken Young and so many more were always there when sales or programming had a problem. They didn't know how to say, "It can't be done." They simply took on the high pressure problem and came up with a solution.

Outstanding among technical people was Alvin Young. He is by far the most talented "audio" man in the city, a fact borne out by 40 years of service to KCMO Radio and television.

I admit I have omitted many who should be mentioned—people who gave something extra, who performed tasks out of their areas of specialization, people who contributed whatever it took to produce a winning team, but who have fallen victim to an author's limited memory. But they know who they are, and their deeds are appreciated.

CHAPTER 79

On the Job

After working in a small station, where everybody learned the hard way what it took to deliver quality programming into thousands of homes, I was now a part of 50,000 watts of power reaching into more than a dozen states. This was big-time radio. KCMO Radio originated play-by-play major league baseball, NFL football, NBA basketball and minor league ice hockey. We also originated Big Eight basketball and football, and even soccer when it became available in the market, not to mention numerous daily sport features. We were *the* sports station!

We in the sales department not only "sold" the sponsors, either directly or through an advertising agency, but often actually served as producers on the broadcasts. A producer in radio, unlike a person bearing the same title in Hollywood, was responsible for all aspects of the broadcast, except for the announcer's duty itself. Seeing that the program went on the air on time, went off on time, and that guests were ready on time was the producer's responsibility, in addition to seeing that commercials were on time, of course. The sales person, or account executive as he was called, enjoyed being associated with the broadcast as a producer. He found being on the scene was extremely important, because it was he who ultimately had to live with

Dick Wall as Manager of KCMO-FM.

the advertiser. In any event, the sales person served as needed.

It became part of my duties, and also my pleasure and privilege, to produce a "fan in the stands with Lynn Faris" segment and the "Locker Room Show" before and after the Kansas City Chiefs football games. I also served in the same capacity on the Kansas City Blues hockey broadcasts. All of it was a part of my sales position.

But two people overshadowed me in the world of production. They were Clotis Barker of sales and George Stump, KCMO program director. Both of them were deeply involved in pro football. Clotis, who came to KCMO from a small market, was a Chiefs' booster from the team's earliest days in Kansas City. A talented young man with a great radio sense, he quickly grasped big time broadcasting. His knowledge of football and his friendship with players, executives and game officials allowed him to become a top flight sports producer. Unfortunately, radio management recognized Clotis' ability and named him manager of our FM operation, which eventually absorbed so much of his time that he gave up sports production.

George Stump, program director, assumed the producer position with all the savvy one could acquire in more than 30 years of radio. For many years, he had been the Dean of Program Directors in Kansas City and had seen most sports. So taking on production of the football programs was a breeze. As it was for him in music, George soon made friends across the country when the Chiefs played at home and on the road. Somehow, since he retired, Chiefs' radio broadcasts just don't seem the same.

Production was only a part of sales, and Joe Hartenbower, Dick Evans and radio sales manager Dick Turner strove to let each person do what he did best.

Jack Jester, another radio veteran, and Joe Lugar, who converted from newspaper to radio with ease, were great. Any account they tackled, they won over. And if service to the client or agency was important, Jack or Joe "owned them." Jack Jester was our King of Service. He knew people, and they loved him.

I personally enjoyed all phases of our sales work. The production was sometimes inconvenient. But all in all, it was a fun time. I loved making cold calls on clients or agency people. And I derived great satisfaction in finding a problem and developing a program or spot schedule to solve it. I met many wonderful people in advertising— many of them remain friends to this day.

Calling It a Day

For more than ten years, I had an opportunity to play on a team with so many great people that it was impossible to experience very many "down" days. Going to work every day under the Tall Tower was like Christmas to me. Great people created a quality product, and I was privileged to take it to an outstanding group of clients and advertising agency men and women. Sometimes they agreed with me and bought the plans. But even those times when they failed to see how I could offer a solution to some of their problems, I was able to deal with first class, sincere people, many of whom are still active in advertising.

Audiences change, problems change, and as younger executives bring new philosophies to the marketplace, one sometimes reaches a point where retirement looks appealing.

As I toyed with the idea of calling it a day, I began to realize what a great group of men and women I had met in the time I represented KCMO Radio, both as an account executive and later as manager of KCMO-FM. I knew that the modest success I enjoyed wasn't the result of any special magic about me. Instead it was a product of the reputation established by KCMO people through personal, telephone or written contacts. All of these created an atmosphere in the advertising community that opened doors for me simply because I was "with KCMO." The warm welcome came from other sources as well. Before there was the abundance of credit cards we know today, I visited most of the restaurants and retail stores in the Kansas City area and was allowed to "sign the check" simply by presenting my business card, without using Visa, American Express, or similar methods of payment. KCMO was the "Open Sesame."

Within the many client organizations and agencies I contacted, the "Tall Tower's" call letters always brought out the welcome mat. And I'm sure that others from our station received the same royal treatment. I enjoyed the friendship of many. Some, like Jack Wheeler, a senior officer with H. O. Peet & Co., entered into only a limited number of advertising programs with us. But I called on him regularly because he was such a fine individual, one from whom I learned something on every visit.

Max Cox and Don Lottman at Southwestern Bell were consistent clients who were great believers in radio. They became wonderful friends who made all of us in the media feel so comfortable. Of course, I always felt that the congeniality in their department of Southwestern Bell began with the warm personality of their administrative assistant, Patty (Pyle) Carlson, who had the knack of making each visitor feel right at home.

The J. Walter Thompson Agency, which handled the Kansas City Ford dealers account, was staffed as professionally as any. Kent Black and Dottie Gallup made advertising a fun thing. Ray Schoenfeld, a crack ad man, worked at the Barrickman Agency and handled many accounts. The most prominent of the Barrickman accounts, to my memory, was Vicker's Oil. Ray was confident, easy to approach and, most importantly, a man with many friends. There were so many more, like Flowers McGuire and Bill Smith (who incidentally married one of KCMO's lovelies, a secretary to George Stump, Linda Calvert). There were people like Bob Bernstein and Skip Rein (who now head one of the top advertising agencies in the nation), Beverly Norman, who was one of Kansas City's most powerful public relations experts and perhaps its most beautiful. And who could forget Pat Paton, a former KCMO-TV floor director who now heads his own very successful advertising and public relations agency. Pat not only has worked at a radio station, but he also now is an owner of one!

John Winchell, who retired as a top executive at TWA, later went on to additional success in a second career as business manager for the Kansas City Blues Hockey Club. In both capacities, he was a good friend to KCMO, and he has remained my close friend ever since. Don Funk, who headed the Bryan Donald Advertising Agency, was also a man of unforgettable quality.

Austin Harmon and John Lee Smith operated Harmon/ Smith Advertising the way it should be done. Classy, all the way! And they both chose Kansas City's only singing barber, Dan Tomaszczuk.

Mention was made of key personnel at KCMO because all of these people from different backgrounds formed a talented staff of communicators, the likes of which is hard to find today. Each was a specialist, but each also dabbled in virtually every facet of broadcasting. Today, from weather people through sports, news, music and even "letter turners," they too often do only one thing. Those I pointed out were able to do it all—and very efficiently for the most part. So while most of these persons are retired or working in other fields, and despite the fact that the names of some who pioneered were omitted due to the writer's faulty memory, they deserve recognition.

So I retired from KCMO and waited for a call to meet new challenges. One day, not too long after settling into retirement, that call came, and new doors opened for me.

I'd really like to devote more words to that subject, but it would require another book.

Say, that's an idea!

Index

Order Form

Please rush _____ copies of **"The Broom Is Out"** by Dick Wall to:

Name _____

Address _____

_____

City/State/Zip _____

Book Price: $19.95.
(2-5 $18.95 ea.; 6 or more $17.95 ea.)

Please Add Shipping/Handling (to the same address):
$4.00 (1 book)
$3.50 per copy (2-5 books)
$3.00 per copy (6 or more books)

Kansas Residents Please Add 6.75% Sales Tax
$1.35 (1 book)
$1.28 per copy (2-5 books)
$1.22 per copy (6 or more books)

Mail Orders:
Leathers Publishing Company
P. O. Box 6108
Leawood, KS 66206

Method of Payment: ❐ money order
❐ check ❐ VISA ❐ MasterCard

Credit Card Orders Call:
Toll Free 1 (888) 888-7696

Credit Card # _____
Expiration Date _____
Cardholder's Signature

_____